D0976598

SELL LIKE AN ACE–
LIVE LIKE A KING!

by JOHN WOLFE

Englewood Cliffs, N.J.
PRENTICE-HALL, INC.

Reward Edition . . . . . . December 1975

Second Printing . . . . . December, 1976

PRINTED IN THE UNITED STATES OF AMERICA

To The Three Around Me

During The Long Nights While This Was Being Written—

My Daughter JANN, who slept . . .

My Wife ALICE, who didn't . . .

And TOPPER, who barked

just enough to keep me awake.

PREFACE

In working with thousands of different salesmen—in every kind of selling—it's always seemed to me that a sales force is a lot like a deck of playing cards.

Whether there are 52 men, or 52 thousand, there are always a bunch at the bottom of the pack—the "deuces" that just can't seem to make the grade. Others, on through the middle, get by—but that's about all. While at the *top* of the pack, backing up the whole organization, there are always a few SELLING ACES.

The ACES, of course, are the fellows who really bring in the business—and bring home the bacon.

For in selling, as in no other line of endeavor, you write your own paycheck. And that's what makes ours such a great profession.

In a factory, if one guy turns out more widgets than his buddy at the next bench, he still draws the same salary. In an office, if one gal types more letters, she still takes home the same money. Our business is different. The more you produce, the more you earn. It's that simple.

Hence, the title of this book: *Sell Like an Ace—Live Like a King!*

Now, a lot of people have an idea that all great salesmen were born that way. Either you've got it or you haven't, they say. Well, don't you believe it! *Please*. Because it just isn't so.

Learning to sell is like learning to swim, or play the piano, or fly an airplane, or anything else. Sure, some fellows happen to have a little more aptitude than others. Maybe they learn quicker. Maybe they even learn better.

But here's Point 1: *Anyone* can learn how.

And Point 2 is even more important: For *everyone*, there's always room for *improvement*.

So whatever your present ability and income level may be— if you want to "Sell Like an Ace and Live Like a King!"— this book is for you.

For here are the techniques that are now earning top dollar for America's top salesmen, every day of the week, every week of the year, all over the country.

As you'll see, these methods cover every step of the sale:

PART I—BEFORE THE SALE, START WITH A SPADE— shows you what to do *before* you meet the prospect face to face, so you'll be able to spend more time in front of more customers, and make that time pay off bigger for you.

PART II—IN EVERY APPROACH, HIT 'EM IN THE HEART—shows you how to capitalize on universal buying instincts, so as to get immediate favorable attention from every prospect you call on.

PART III—WHEN DEMONSTRATING, DEAL IN DIA-MONDS—shows you how to *prove* that your product or service is the one to buy, how to put real power into every presentation.

PART IV—TO CLINCH THE CLOSE, CUSHION 'EM WITH A CLUB—shows you easy *low*-pressure ways to answer every objection you run into, and how to get the signature on the dotted line.

PART V—THE JOKER—DO IT—covers the "you" in selling, showing you in specific terms how *you* can harness this power of the Aces for your own benefit, to help *you* start right now to "Sell Like an Ace—Live Like a King!"

In other words, the book is *complete*. And that's important.

For if there's one all-inclusive, overriding fact I've noticed in watching all these Selling Aces operate, it's this: The true Selling Ace does *everything* right! He doesn't goof on *any* part of the sale. He can't afford to. Because in selling, as in mountain climbing, one misstep is one too many.

So it makes no difference where your own particular strengths or weaknesses may lie. This book is designed to help you sharpen up *every* phase of your selling—all the way from finding the prospect to taking his money.

It doesn't matter *what* you sell, either. You'll find specific examples for industrial equipment, consumer products, specialty items, intangibles—everything that's sold. Plus a lot of other potent ideas that apply in *all* fields.

And this I can tell you for sure: these methods *work*. I know. I've seen the results. All *you* have to do is *put* them to work!

So, for all these reasons, I think it will pay you to come along with me for a while.

There's just one more thing I want to mention before we get started.

This isn't the usual dry sort of "text book" on selling. It's not designed as entertainment, of course—making money is, for most people, a serious business. But, at the same time, the medicine is liberally sugar-coated. Take it in easy doses and I think you'll enjoy it.

As I've said, nothing in these pages will do you any good at all unless you *do* something about it—that's the Joker in the deal.

But first you have to read the book.

P. S.

The words you've just read were written several years ago, before this book first went to press.

Now, as another printing is about to come out, one essential truth emerges, clear and unalterable: the more that things change in this business of selling, the more they stay the same.

The selling profession has grown in stature, as more and more people have come to realize that *distribution* (not production) is what keeps the wheels of our economy turning, and gives Americans the highest standard of living ever known.

Hundreds of additional companies, and many thousands more salesmen, have found the Selling Aces a sure-fire key to increased sales and greater profits. Our Selling Aces Workshops are now conducted in major cities across the nation and around the world, bringing a brighter future to more and more success-minded men and women every year. To the individual who *uses* these tested techniques, the rewards are greater than ever.

And that's the only Joker—which will always remain in the deck. It's still up to you.

CONTENTS

Part I

BEFORE THE SALE, START WITH A SPADE

Part III

WHEN DEMONSTRATING, DEAL IN DIAMONDS

Part IV

TO CLINCH THE CLOSE, CUSHION 'EM WITH A CLUB

Part V

THE JOKER—DO IT

PART I

Selling Ace #1
BEFORE THE SALE

START WITH A
SPADE

Chapter 1

YOU HAVE TO KNOW
BEFORE YOU CROW

People Like to Listen to Authorities

Let's start this off with the bare fundamentals.

Naturally, I hope this book is going to be read by a lot of people. Some are going to be raw beginners at this game of selling. Others will have worlds of experience. Exactly where *you* fit in on the scale, of course, I don't know.

But regardless of how much you know about selling now, I'm pretty sure you'll know a good deal more, long before you reach the last page. Because, by the time we're through, we'll have analyzed all the finer points—the subtle techniques that are bound to help you close the tough sales as well as the easy ones.

But you have to start with the basics—so that's what we're going to do.

And the very first rule is: *know what you're talking about.*

Why? Because people buy from salesmen they trust, and people trust authorities. It's that simple.

Years ago, that wasn't always true. We've all heard tales of glib "super-salesmen" who could charm unsuspecting buyers into ordering their merchandise. According to legend, these men didn't know anything except how to talk. Maybe so.

But today, with all the mass media of communication, folks are pretty well informed. And if you want to sell 'em, you have to be *better* informed than they are! That's the only way you'll ever be able to convince 'em.

So whatever you sell—whatever business you're in—become an *authority* on that subject. If yours is a tangible product, learn about its manufacture, study its uses. If you sell an intangible service, become an expert on it.

Remember, every piece of product knowledge is like a parachute: you may get along O.K. without it, but when you need it—Brother, you need it!

Joe Salesman, M.D.

Have you ever thought of yourself as an M.D.? Probably not, but that's what I'm going to suggest. Because just knowing the *product* (or service) is not enough. You've got to be a doctor as well.

What do I mean?

Well, think for just a minute about your own family physician. There's a man who can sell you almost anything! Not just because he sells a mighty important product—which he does. And not just because he knows the construction of the human body—which I'm sure he does. Not even because he's an authority on any one illness—which he well may be.

It's because he's an authority on *all* your medical needs. When you feel sick, you go to him, confident that he can *solve your problem*.

There's the answer! Your family doctor isn't really a salesman at all—he's a *problem-solver!* That's why you buy from him.

And there's a clue as to how you can get more people to buy from *you*. Just become a problem-solver!

This means you have to become an expert on *everything* connected with your business—and, as much as possible, an expert on your prospect's business as well.

So if you sell office supplies, study office procedures. If you sell industrial equipment, bone up on factory operations. If you sell merchandise for resale, learn how your customers can best resell it.

Essentially, it's simply a matter of putting yourself in the other fellow's shoes.

When we opened our Southwest Office in Houston recently, we decided to brighten up the walls with a few paintings. We visited several shops. They all carried somewhat similar paintings, all offered approximately the same values, and their salesmen all seemed familiar with the products they were selling Somehow, we didn't buy.

That is, until we met a problem-solver, the owner of a small, rather dingy store on the edge of town.

This fellow didn't talk about his paintings at all. He talked about our new office! He asked how large the rooms were, the color of the walls, how the furniture would be arranged, even the nature of our business. Only then, on the basis of this information, did he recommend a few paintings—and he was able to tell us intelligently *why* he made those specific recommendations. Naturally, he got the order.

So why not become an M.D. and put those initials after *your name*—in your own mind if not on your business card?

What do the initials stand for? *Doctor of Marketing!*

Just another word for problem-solver. They mean the same thing—and they mean more sales for you.

What to Do When You Don't Know

I can answer that one in two words: admit it!

This may seem like something of a paradox. For, as we've discussed, you *should* know all the answers. If you do, the situation will never develop. And, because knowing all the answers is so important, you don't want to admit any lack of knowledge. The prospect is bound to lose confidence in you to some extent.

But the point is, he's going to lose *more* confidence if you try to fool him! Because you won't get away with it.

You may know the rule they use in the Army: Always give the enemy credit for as much intelligence as yourself. Now, of course, prospects are never, never our enemies—they just

---

act like it. But they *are* intelligent. Try to bluff your way out of a situation and they're bound to catch you at it.

What happens then? The prospect loses confidence in everything else you say. That one weak link will break your whole chain of selling.

So if you don't know the answer to a question, say so in just those words: "Sorry, I don't know."

Of course, sometimes you can minimize the importance of the unknown fact by emphasizing another point.

If you were selling rope, for instance, and you couldn't answer a question regarding the number of strands woven into it, you might say: "Sorry, I really don't know—but it's guaranteed to take a 1000 pound load!"

And there's one more thing you can do: find out! Then you won't get stuck on that question the next time.

Chapter 1 in a Nutshell

1. People trust authorities—that's why they buy from 'em.
2. Become an M.D.—a Doctor of Marketing.
3. If you **don't** know, say so—and find out.

Chapter 2

HOW TO LICK COMPETITION

The Buying Spiral

I don't suppose there ever lived a salesman who didn't worry about his competition. If So-and-so didn't have those new models, if the buyers would stop demanding that other brand, if they'd just quit chiseling on price, etc., etc., etc., things would be so different. Without *them* life would be so sweet!

But here's the funny thing: those **#**#**©#©© competitors are just as worried about *you* as you are of them—or at least they will be if you put this book to work!

Because competition is like the Income Tax—you can't get away from it.

Actually, you've probably got a lot more competition than you realize, and that's where this Buying Spiral comes in. What it means, essentially, is that everything competes with everything.

Here's why.

In the last analysis, the only time anybody buys anything is when he decides he'd rather have that particular thing than the money he pays for it. And, obviously, if he didn't buy it he could use that money to buy something else—*anything* else.

We were out with our friends the Otto Norvigs the other evening—he's Sales Manager for the Buell Corporation. They mentioned that they were about to buy either a new car, or a boat, or a swimming pool, or a trip to Europe. Talk about competition! I'll bet the auto salesman they're talking to doesn't know he's battling a boat dealer, a swimming pool builder, and a travel agent. But he is.

And that's not at all unusual. Remember this fact: whenever you call on a prospect, you are competing against *everybody*—not just your "competitors" who happen to be selling the same type of item.

Specifically, then, the Buying Spiral means this:

Every buyer—of any product or service—climbs a sort of mental circular staircase. He starts off at the bottom with a certain amount of money to be spent anywhere in the marketplace. He climbs a few steps and decides to spend that money in one of several ways. Then he climbs a little higher and narrows his choice down to just a few kinds of products. A bit higher still, he makes up his mind as to the *one* product or service he is going to buy—and only *then* does he start to decide which *brand* of that product or service he'll pick.

If you want to check this, just tune in to any popular TV quiz show. When the big prize is won and the applause subsides, the M.C. invariably asks: "Well, what do you plan to do with all that money?" Sometimes he gets a definite answer. But usually the winning contestant has to think about it. He hasn't even *begun* to think about brands—he still has to decide on the *kind* of product he wants most. Because—with money—he can buy *anything*.

The Big Green Giant and How to Kill It

So far, this sounds like a tough situation. You've always known you had competition from other outfits in the same business. Now—and perhaps for the first time—you find out that you're competing against other *kinds* of businesses, too.

But, in another sense, I've really narrowed down the competition for you.

Because, you see, all of this means you have just one competitor—*money*. Like everybody else—like it or not—you're fighting for that Great American Dollar, and that's the *only* competition you've got.

So that dollar bill is the Big Green Giant you have to kill. Here's how.

The first step we've already covered. That's the realization that *it* is only your only real competition.

The next step is to figure out what your product offers *exclusively*—the advantages of your product over *anything* else. Naturally, this requires a thorough knowledge of what you're selling, and a knowledge of the entire industry as well. That's why I emphasized this so strongly in Chapter 1.

This may mean you'll have to widen your sights a little.

At the New England Sales Management Conference in Boston a couple of years ago, I had the pleasure of sharing the platform with Walter Johnson, Vice-President of American Airlines. He pointed out in his speech how the airlines had built such a huge volume of business in only a few years. Most of this traffic, he said, consisted of people who formerly rode trains and busses. But today, he claimed, the airlines are shooting for a far greater market—they're going after the folks who now vacation in their cars.

What Walter Johnson meant was that his firm had to sell travel first, airline travel second, and third—finally—American Airlines.

You have to do the same thing. Sell the basic product first —then sell your particular brand.

The third step in killing the Big Green Giant is simply this: *you have to make what you're selling worth more in the prospect's mind than the money it costs.*

It would take a whole book to tell you how to do that.

This is the book.

Don't Tear 'Em Down—Let 'Em Fall

But, you're probably saying, what happens *after* the prospect has settled down to deciding on your particular type of product or service. He's ruled out all the other uses for his money. He wants the kind of thing you have to sell. How do you convince him that *yours* is the brand he ought to buy?

That's simple: you tell him yours is better!

But there are, essentially, two ways to do that. One's right and one's wrong. Of course, selling is not an exact science, and the tactics you use must often be determined by the particular situation. Here's one place, however, where the lines are clearly drawn. This is strictly a matter of black and white. There's no gray in between.

The wrong way is to tell your prospect why the other fellow's product is bad. The right way is to tell him why yours is good.

This may seem like a fine distinction. It is, of course, a relative matter, but there's a world of difference between these two approaches. Actually, your handling of this touchy problem may easily affect the entire outcome of your presentation. Either you make the sale—or you don't.

Let's analyze it.

First of all, your product probably *isn't* so darn much better than the other fellow's. Nobody has a corner on productive genius. The guy who designs or makes the competitor's product is pretty smart, too. And your prospect knows it.

So if you say, "Theirs is no good," or "It's just a pile of junk," or "They're a bunch of chiselers," two things happen: first, the prospect begins to think maybe the competition *does* have something worthwhile to offer; second, he is apt to mistrust everything else you say.

As Shakespeare pointed out, there's a danger in protesting too much.

When I was a kid of about twelve, someone gave me a set of magic tricks. In one of the stunts, a ring was threaded onto a length of string, and then, while both ends of the string were tightly held by a spectator, the ring was mysteriously removed. One day I eagerly tried this one out on my dad. After completing the trick I proudly said, "You see, there's only one ring!" "Ah hah!" said my dad, who, like most prospects, was never very stupid. "That must be the answer. You had two rings; otherwise, you wouldn't have brought up the matter!" And, of course, he was right. As usual.

When you emphasize a point too strongly, the other fellow is going to wonder why—usually to your disadvantage.

So don't—*ever*—knock your competition. It isn't nice. It isn't smart.

But, instead, if you the let the prospect discover for *himself* that the other product is inferior, it's very nice—and very smart.

Again, you do this by giving your prospect the *exclusive* advantages he'll enjoy in your product or service.

And to do that, obviously, *you* have to know what those exclusive advantages are.

That's why you have to Start with a Spade.

Uniqueness—With a Capital "You"

Occasionally you find yourself in a spot where, admittedly, your competition has the edge. Maybe the other fellow's product *is* better—which, let's face it, can happen. Or perhaps his line is more widely advertised than yours. Point for point, product-wise, you have less to offer. You know it and your prospect knows it. It's a tough spot to be in.

Or possibly you sell a commodity where every brand is pretty much the same, where there are no competitive advantages one way or the other. That's just as bad.

You still have one exclusive feature *no one* else can offer—and it's the most important thing you'll ever sell.

No doubt you've already guessed what this exclusive item is. Sure—it's *you*. Because there's nothing else in the world like *you*.

As I say, this is important. It's so important, in fact, that the entire final Part of this book is devoted to the "you" in selling. But right now, while we're talking about competitive advantages, it certainly deserves mention.

So remember, no one else has *your* particular personality; *your* service to the customer is something only *you* can offer; and *you* are the only one who can deliver what *you* promise.

When the prospect wants *you*, there's only one place he can get it—from *you*.

Chapter 2 in a Nutshell

1. Everyone has to compete—against everyone else.
2. Your product has to be worth more than just one thing—money.
3. Don't knock your competition. Let 'em knock themselves—out.
4. You are you-nique.

Chapter 3

KEEP YOUR EYE ON THE
PROSPECT DOLLAR SIGN

It Takes Two to Make a Deal

So far, in Part I, we've been talking about the product you
sell. As we've seen, that's mighty important. Knowing that
product inside and out is a big part of what I mean by "Starting with a Spade."

Now we come to the next step—and it's just as important.
That's the *prospect* you sell.

Because, I think we can agree, it takes two to make a deal.

You can take the best product in the world, give it to the
best salesman in the world, and send that Selling Ace with
that product down to some desert island surrounded by nothing
but water. Result? No sales. There never are—without *prospects*.

By the way, some salesmen have told me that their territories
are just about as barren as that desert island! But it isn't so.
There are always prospects to be found, and finding them is
a big part of your job.

Without *prospects*, you'll never sell anything.

Don't Make Calls—Make Sales

This may seem like another paradox. Because if you don't
make calls, you certainly won't make sales.

13

But the important thing is *where* you call and on *whom*.

The answer is that you have to tell your story to the right people. You have to call on real live *prospects*. Your time is limited, and you have to spend it where it will pay off in sales volume.

Of course, there are some fields where the "buckshot" technique must be used. That's where you sell a comparatively inexpensive item, usually a specialty, and you can't tell in advance who is likely to buy it. You have to try to sell everybody.

One of my own first jobs in selling was for a radio publicity outfit that was running a promotion for Station KSFO in San Francisco. My job was to sell participation in the program to businessmen—the more the merrier—for $39.50.

The boss went through the classified section of the telephone book and made cards for *every* firm in the San Francisco Bay area. Phone calls were made to each and every company, and the entire sales presentation to each firm was completed over the phone in about ten minutes. It was impossible to predict who might buy the deal, so this was probably the best way to go about selling that particular product. And, I was happy to find out, it worked!

But that's a somewhat unusual situation. Normally—and this is most probably true in your case—you *decide* where, how, and with whom you spend your selling time and effort.

And the only way to do that intelligently is to be just plain mercenary about it. There's really only one sign you have to watch for—the dollar sign.

Then measure that sign against the time it takes you to make it pay off.

You may discover, for instance, that you'll build the biggest total volume by making a lot of little sales, rather than wasting time angling for the big kill. Or, on the other hand, you may find that you can sell the big ones just as easily and quickly as the small ones. That's something you'll have to learn for yourself.

The important thing is to make calls that will make sales that will make dollars.

They've Got to Qualify

You've probably heard a lot about qualifying prospects. Obviously, if you're going to follow the advice I've been handing out here, you'd better learn how to do it. Because the quicker you can find out whether or not the man *does* qualify as a prospect, the more sales and dollars you'll make.

Personally, I've always felt that there are just three all-important questions that need to be answered. If the answer to any of them—any *one* of them—is no, you'd better pack your bag and exit gracefully. If your man passes all three tests, stick with him and sell. He's a prospect.

Here they are.

1. *Does he need it?* We've all heard about selling ice boxes to Eskimos. Maybe it's possible. I don't know. But I *do* know that a man who doesn't need something isn't apt to buy it. He may need it and not *know* that he needs it—that's O.K. You can tell him! But the basic need has to be there.

Here again, you may sell a product like insurance that is needed by everyone. But even there, the need varies from one man to the next. How recently has his insurance program been analyzed? What changes have taken place in his family or financial situation? The answers to questions like these determine the extent of the need, and, therefore, the speed with which you can reasonably anticipate positive action.

Often, it's more clear-cut. Either the man needs your product or he doesn't.

When I first got out of college, I was offered a job with a Sonotone Hearing Aid agency. This firm recognized the importance of discovering the need. As it was explained to me, many folks who need hearing aids don't want them, but unless someone *does* need a hearing aid he certainly won't buy one.

My assignment (which, by the way, I didn't accept) was simply to dig out the prospects. I was supposed to canvass the area and, at each home, ask a question. If I got an answer, I was to leave, without making any note of the house. If, on the other hand, the woman cupped a hand over one ear and said, "Eh?" then I was supposed to write the number of the house on a prospect card!

That may seem a little silly, and, actually, the method was a little more involved than I have indicated. But it does point up the true basic fact: you have to uncover a *need* for your product before you can sell it.

2. *Can he buy it?* Usually, it isn't too hard to get someone to listen to your story. If you make a reasonably good impression, you can probably get a hearing without too much trouble.

The big question is: are you being heard by the right person? If not, again, you're probably wasting your time.

This applies especially when you sell to big companies. There may be 1000 men in a firm who have the authority to say "No" to you, and only one who can say "Yes." That *one* is the prospect. The others aren't.

And some of these others can be very nice fellows. They'll tell you: "My recommendations carry a lot of weight," or, "Let me carry the ball and I'll sell it upstairs," or, "Don't worry about it, I just have to get the boss's O.K."

Don't be lured into this trap! As I say, these are nice fellows. But they're poison. Chances are, unintentionally, they'll kill your deal. *You* are the salesman and the *boss* is the buyer. You have to talk to *him*.

In Chapter 7 we'll take a look at some of the techniques successful Selling Aces use to get to the right man.

By the way, this same principle applies even in direct-to-consumer selling. The Encyclopedia Americana, for instance, trains its salespeople never to talk to either the husband or the wife alone. Knowing that an investment of that kind is normally undertaken by both heads of the family *together*, the Americana folks insist on talking to *both*. And, of course, if either the husband *or* the wife is in sole supreme command, by getting both together they can't miss!

3. *Can he pay for it?* Ah, there's a question! For if any non-prospect is nicer than the man who has no power to buy, it's the man who has no power to pay!

Here, again, we're talking about that filthy stuff called money. Awful, isn't it?

But the only sales that do you any good are the sales that are profitable for your company. And the only profitable sales are the ones that are paid for. If the man you're talking to can't *pay* for what he buys, run! He's worse than the guy who doesn't buy at all. Much worse.

If your credit manager doesn't accept the order, you're in trouble. If he does, you're both in trouble.

And—I'll say it just once more—no one makes any money.

Those, then, are the three tests that must be passed before you can call a man a real live prospect. If you can get the answers to these questions before you make the call, so much the better. In that case, you may not make it. If you can't, then get them as early as possible in the interview. Don't waste any more time than you have to.

If you were perfect—and, of course, no one is—you would never open your mouth (sales-wise) to anyone except a real live *prospect*.

Chapter 3 in a Nutshell

1. It takes two to make a deal. You need a **prospect**.
2. Watch for the sign—the sign of the dollar.
3. If he:
     (a) needs it,
     (b) can buy it,
     (c) can pay for it,
   then he's a prospect.

Chapter 4

LOOK FOR THE
ACRES OF DIAMONDS

Prospects Are Where You Find Them

In Chapter 3 we discussed the vital importance of the prospect in your scheme of selling, and we took a look at some of the yardsticks by which you can measure the quality of each prospect you call on.

But even before you qualify 'em, you've got to *find* 'em. So now let's talk about that.

Here again, of course, the importance of continually coming up with *new* prospects varies according to your own business, and the particular kind of selling it calls for.

If, for instance, you sell a line of merchandise to wholesalers or retailers for resale to others, you've most probably got a list of accounts you regularly call on and service. You open a new one whenever you can, but you spend most of your time selling as much as you can to the accounts already on the books. If you sell industrial components, the same is apt to hold true.

If, on the other hand, you sell insurance, automobiles, or almost any specialty item, then prospecting for new customer-blood is a big part of your job. Here, you don't really have "accounts" at all—once you've got yourself a customer you have to turn around and find another. Which is one of the reasons why this kind of selling is usually the most rewarding—if you know how to do it.

But—in either case—you're bound to need *some* new ones. Otherwise you're apt to stand still. And once you do that, you're sure to start going backwards.

And the first rule for finding new prospects is simply this: they're where you find 'em. Which is just a way of saying that there's never any *one* place to look. Remember, your next hot prospect may—right now—be anywhere. He may show up where you least expect. It's your job to dig him out.

Here's what this means.

In Chapter 3 I pointed out the importance of *qualifying* your prospects. If the man doesn't meet specifications, you don't want to waste time on him.

But you should never rule out a prospect just because you *think* he won't measure up. You'll never know for sure until you find out!

I remember when I first learned to fly, right after World War II. The field was an old abandoned military strip on Oahu, on the other side of the Island from Honolulu. There were five flying schools along that strip, all doing a land-office business, thanks to the G.I. Bill, and all flying (and supposedly selling) different makes of private airplanes. None of the students looked very much like prospective airplanes owners, and I'm sure I was no exception. So no one ever approached me about buying.

Until one day I casually met the owner of one of these five outfits. This man, it turned out, didn't just run a flying school. He was a *businessman*—and a *salesman*. He made it a point to find out three things about me: (1) being in a business that required me to travel throughout the Islands, I did have a *need* for an airplane; (2) being my own boss, I had the *authority* to make a decision; and (3) I had the *money* to pay for it.

P.S. I bought an airplane.

P.P.S. I'm glad I did!

One of our clients is the Investors Planning Corporation, a most successful organization dealing in mutual funds. One of their top men was telling me recently about his newborn son. After extolling the wonders of his remarkable offspring, he added: "Of course, while I was at the hospital visiting my wife and the baby, I also sold investment plans to the doctor, the nurse, and two interns!"

Just one word of caution here. It's important to have customers, but it's also important to have friends. You're proud of your product, or you wouldn't be selling it, and it's perfectly O.K.—as well as good business—to let everyone know what you're selling. But don't overdo it. You'll have more customers —*and* more friends—if you play it cool.

How to Hunt with Bird Dogs

Possibly the only thing wrong with your profession is that selling is a one-man business. (Of course, when you're sharp enough, you'll be a sales manager with other fellows working under you, so that will fix that!) But right now, as a team of one man, you're strictly on your own. Every time a sale is made, *you* have to be there to make it. Even if your customers send in re-orders direct, which you get credit for, it's still as a result of *your* efforts.

But there's one phase of selling where you can multiply yourself like a rabbit. This is it. And because—in prospecting— you *can* become a whole army, you most decidedly ought to take advantage of the opportunity.

Because, if other people can't do your selling for you, they *can* help you find prospects. Just as in hunting, while the man with the gun is the only one who can shoot the birds, the *bird dog* can show him where they are.

The next question, obviously, is: where do you find the bird dogs? And the answer to that one is *everywhere*. Besides, unlike the prospects, the people who help you *find* the prospects don't have to qualify in any way at all! All they have to do is *want* to help you!

Another point: while your friends may sometimes resent your trying to sell *them*, they'll rarely object to helping you sell someone *else!*

This means you can enlist the aid of your wife, your family, your friends, your doctor or lawyer, your barber—anyone and everyone. Just ask 'em to help you find prospects—and they will. Naturally, this depends again on what you sell and who your prospects are. But no matter what you sell—or to whom—you can almost always latch onto prospects in this way.

So far, we've been talking about "amateur" bird dogs—the folks who help you find prospects just because they like you and want to. Usually, they're the best kind!

But not always. Again, depending on your line of business, you may be able to *hire* bird dogs.

One of the most successful automobile salesmen I've ever met—who is in many ways strictly an average salesman—has a team of twenty-seven paid bird dogs. They include a druggist, a newsstand operator, a hardware dealer, several service station attendants, etc., etc. This Selling Ace has a standard deal with each one: for every lead that results in a sale, the bird dog gets a twenty-dollar bill. And it works!

A slightly subdued version of this same system is used along Madison Avenue. When an advertising agent helps a public relations firm land an account, or when a printer steers a client toward the advertising agency, there is often a "gentlemen's agreement" that a "finder's fee" will be paid. And I've seldom heard of the fee being refused!

Please bear in mind that I am not talking about "paying off" a buyer for placing business with you. That's a poisonous practice, and I don't approve of it—ever. In the long run, it's bound to hurt.

But when someone *on the outside* gives you a lead that results in business for you, some tangible expression of appreciation is perfectly in order. If nothing else, a bottle of liquor. (Or a case, depending on the size of the order and the thirst of the bird dog!)

The Chain Letter Principle

Here's another method of finding prospects that really works wonders. It operates on the same principle used in the old chain letters—with just one exception. In a chain letter almost everyone loses (which is why the courts ruled them illegal). This system of prospecting is strictly according to Hoyle—and everyone wins! Especially you.

And all you need to start it going is *one* customer. Here's how.

After you finish working with that one customer—assuming he's satisfied—you ask him for the names of other folks you might call on. Let's say he gives you enough names to net you just *two* more customers. That's not very many, is it?

But then let's say you do the same thing with those two, and you get the same very-much-within-reason result. Now you've got *four* more customers. Repeat this once more, and you've got *eight* more. Another repeat, you've got *sixteen* more. And so it goes: 32, 64, 128, 256, 512, 1024, 2048, 4096, 8192.

After just fifteen "generations" of calls, you'll have over *sixteen thousand* new red hot prospects to call on! And this is *after* you've *sold* the *other sixteen thousand* during the previous fourteen "generations"!

In fact—mathematically—if you went through this same procedure just fifteen times more, you would have sold darn near every man, woman and child in the *world!* Honest! That's the way it works out.

Of course, there's just a *slight* chance it won't work out quite this well in actual practice! For lots of reasons that are as obvious to me as they are to you.

But the principle *does* work.

The Nutri-Bio Corporation has built one of the largest food supplement businesses in the world, mainly through the use of this system. Each salesperson is provided with special cards to give to each customer, on which the names of other prospective customers are listed. Each of *those* customers provides more names, etc., etc.

But whether you use formalized cards or simply doodle the information in a notebook, the results are the same—and they can be terrific.

Remember, just *one* customer, two customers, four. . . . wheeee! Away we go!

Your Best Prospects Are Customers

Maybe this doesn't belong in this chapter. Because, over the last few pages, we've been talking strictly about *new* prospects. Now we're not.

But, nevertheless, this is a point that too many salesmen forget. And it's important.

As we said at the start, every business—and every sales territory—constantly needs new blood pumped into it, in the form of new customers.

But the *amount* of new blood needed is directly proportional to the amount *lost* through improper—or insufficient—selling.

Maybe yours is a field where every sale is a one-shot proposition. Once a man is a customer, you can't sell him anything else—ever. If so, this doesn't apply to you. *All* your customers are new ones.

But if your success depends on *repeat* business, then remember: your present customers are your best prospects.

For two reasons.

First, if a man is already your customer, it's easier to sell him again. You don't have to go through the preliminaries. But you *do* have to continue to cultivate his good will, and that's the point I want to make. Sometimes salesmen get too cocky about a customer—they figure they've got him sewed up. But that's just the time someone else comes along and offers that *extra* service or attention, and you lose out. What else can you expect? That's the way *you* worked to get him in the first place!

Second, if a man is already buying from you, it's usually easier to sell him *more* than it is to open a new account. So don't be satisfied until you feel sure that you're getting *all* the business you can from each account you now serve. If you double your volume with a present account, that's just like opening a new one!

So in looking for *new* customers, don't forget the old ones. Thar's more gold in *them* thar hills, too!

Chapter 4 in a Nutshell

1. A prospect is like your mouth—you can't see it because it's right under your nose!
2. Let others do the spotting, so you can do more selling.
3. Prospects make prospects make prospects make prospects make prospects.
4. It's easy to lose business—but just as easy to keep it.

Chapter 5

THE SUREST WAY
TO DOUBLE YOUR SALES

How Much Is Your Time Worth?

Right now you may be wondering when we'll get into the actual sale itself. Enough of the preliminaries, you may be saying, let's get on with the main event.

Well, that's the whole point of this chapter.

Because the "main event"—when you're face to face with the prospect—is the *only* time you make any money. And that makes it mighty important.

So the purpose of this chapter is to help you increase your selling time. In later chapters we'll cover all the techniques you can use to win the main event once you're in it. Right now let's talk about how to get into more bouts, how to use more *time* for actual selling.

I wonder if you know how much this time is really worth —to *you* that is—in dollars and cents. If not, now would be a good time to find out.

There are just two things you have to determine: (1) how much time do you spend now in face-to-face selling? and (2) what is your average weekly or monthly paycheck?

The second is something you already know. The first, you probably don't.

So right now I'm going to suggest that you keep a record for a few weeks. A regular time check. For each day, of each week, mark down the number of hours and minutes you spend actually talking to prospects and customers. Not waiting time. Not traveling time. Not social time. (And not the few minutes it will take you to keep the record!) Figure in only the time you spend *selling*.

You may be surprised! Various surveys, in different fields, have shown the average salesman's selling time to be no more than one to three hours a day! That's all. But you have to find out what it is in *your own* case.

Then simply divide your weekly hours into your weekly earnings. And that's it. That's how much *your* selling time is worth to *you*.

If, for instance, your actual selling time amounts to ten hours a week, and you earn $100 during that week, your time is worth $10 an hour. If you average only five selling hours a week, and you net $200 per, then your time is worth $40 an hour.

However it works out, I'll bet your time is a lot more valuable than you thought. *Too valuable to waste!*

Watch the Clock

Now let's see just how to avoid wasting this precious asset called time. Because, obviously, if you increase your selling time, you increase your sales. If you can double your productive hours, this won't affect your hourly wage. But it *will* double your *sales!*

The first step is to realize just how important this time is— and that you've already done.

The next step is simply to eliminate doing the things that cost you time without earning you money.

Let's say, for instance, that your hourly pay rate worked out to $20 an hour.

This means that an hour lunch costs you $20, a half-hour late start in the morning costs you $10, and even a fifteen-minute coffee break costs you a 5 spot. That's $35 out of your pocket right there!

Now, I'm not suggesting you go without lunch, never stop

for gas, or neglect your physical needs. Obviously, that's silly.

But you *can* cut down on these time-wasters.

If it's appropriate in your business, for instance, take customers to lunch as often as possible. The price of the meal is a lot less than the $20 taken out of your pocket when you eat alone. When you do eat alone, make it a quickie.

Start earlier in the morning. The Osborne-Kemper-Thomas Company, manufacturers of advertising specialties, believes in this principle—and practices it. The executive offices of the firm open at 8:00 A.M. each morning, rather than the customary 9:00 o'clock. Salesmen are instructed to follow suit—and they profit by it.

Don't wait too long to see a buyer. Unless there's an unusually good reason, limit your waiting time to ten minutes. As we point out in our Workshops around the country, waiting too long ruins your prestige and makes it harder for you to make the sale, as well as wasting time. If you send word in to the buyer that you can't wait but will be glad to come back later, usually you'll get in without further delay.

Try to make a "bonus" call every day. After each day's calls are completed, make one more. This "extra" call means extra sales.

Now for the third basic step in increasing your selling time. It's simply this: *make more calls at the wrong time!*

If that sounds screwy, let me explain.

Naturally, timing is important in selling, just as in everything else. You should *try* to make every call at the precise moment when the buyer is most apt to be in, and in a buying mood. (We'll get into planning later in this chapter.)

But the fact is you can't! It's just plain impossible for every call to be timed perfectly. And if you insist on limiting your selling to ideal conditions, you'll just be limiting your selling. Period.

So go ahead! Make a few calls "too early" in the morning! Bother people when they're "on their way out to lunch!" Drop in just as they're leaving for the day! Make 'em miss their first martini!

You might make a few folks temporarily annoyed. You *will* make more sales!

Put Away the Calendar

This is sort of a long-range view of what we've just been talking about. After all, your *weekly* earnings are really unimportant. You're interested in how you make out for the whole year. You want to eat *every* week.

So you have to sell the same way. Every week. Every month. Every day.

Here again, it's awfully easy to fall into the mental rut of deciding that at certain times of the year it's impossible to sell anything.

And the buyers seldom try to change that opinion!

Right after the first of the year there's inventory. Then everyone's away on vacation. When they get back they're too busy to see anyone. Next they're tied up in meetings. Then they're out of town. All summer they're away. And so it goes until December, and everyone knows you can't sell anything *then!*

Nuts!

The next time a prospect tells you he isn't buying anything "this month" ask him if he wants to stop selling *his* product!

This happened to my friend Kei Yamato, head of a very successful promotional firm in New York called Orchids of Hawaii. Kei was trying to set up a promotion deal with one of the big soap firms at one time, and he was getting the "put-off" from his prospect, who told Kei they "weren't doing anything just now."

"Oh, really?" asked Kei Yamato. "Aren't folks taking baths this season?" (He got the deal.)

Of course, some businesses are seasonal by nature. If you sell motorboats in Maine, chances are that fall and winter will be slack seasons for you. Snow tires move slowly in spring and summer.

But even strictly seasonal goods can be sold year-round through smart merchandising.

Frank Titelman, President of Puritan Sportswear, told me

how his firm got the jump on competition by offering fall sweaters to the trade in the spring for fall delivery.

Alcort, Inc., of Waterbury, Connecticut, manufactures the Sailfish, a sailing surfboard—obviously a seasonal item. But by giving a small model of the Sailfish with each order placed during the "off" months, Alcort's dealers make sales all year round. Every year that model can be found under thousands of Christmas trees!

The important thing to remember is this: whatever you sell *can* be sold *all* the time. Maybe in varying amounts—no business remains static. But *some* can be sold.

And if you're going to increase your sales for the *year*, you've got to increase them—on the average—every day of every week of every month.

All you have to do is increase the *time* you spend on the job.

Make Up a Sales Time-Table

Now that you've increased your selling time to the maximum, the next step is to make sure you spend it wisely. It must be *planned*.

For in selling—as in living—you have to decide where you want to go. And then you have to *go* there.

One of the most remarkable young men in America is Earl Nightingale, who decided he was going to retire at the age of 35—and earned enough money to do just that. In a recent talk at the New York Sales Executives Club, Earl Nightingale compared people to ships. No ship ever sails around the world, he said. First it has to cross one specific ocean, and land at one particular port. Then it moves on to the next port, and then the next, and so on. It can't go everywhere at once. And unless its course is charted properly in advance, it never arrives anywhere.

Too many people, he said, start life blindly. They don't know where they're going, so they never get there.

Now, this can be narrowed down to each month, each week, each day of your selling career. Not only can—*must*.

Have *you* ever made up a real sales time-table? If not, now's the time to do it.

Basically, your time-table should meet two requirements: (1) it must call for a rough, fast schedule, with near-perfect timing; but (2) the schedule must be feasible.

The airlines offer a good example. If a major airline advertised transcontinental service of, say, twenty-four hours, there wouldn't be many customers—all the competition, offering faster schedules, would get all the business. On the other hand, if the airline promised Coast-to-Coast flights in, say, ten minutes, this would put the line out of business, too, because the schedule couldn't be met.

So what you want is the fastest possible schedule—but it's got to be *possible*.

And, of course, unlike the airlines, you want to figure as many stops as you can.

Again, this depends on the kind of sales presentation you have to make. In various kinds of engineering sales, and in certain other situations where an entire line must be shown, an adequate presentation requires a couple of hours. In that case, obviously, you can't figure more than two or three presentations a day. Other kinds of products can be sold quickly, and more stops can be scheduled.

Another factor is the size of your territory. The more time needed to travel, obviously, the fewer stops you can make.

But this again points up the value of scheduling. For if the territory is properly analyzed, and the schedule is intelligently planned, you can arrange calls so as to minimize traveling time, and hence make more calls.

So, looking at the territory, and analyzing the prospects you want to see, plan a time-table for each day that will enable you to see the most people. It's the only way to make sure you make the most sales possible.

One of our clients is the Four Roses Distillers Company—and I like *their* product about as well as any I've worked with! At any rate, each Four Roses salesman is assigned a territory including several hundred taverns and package stores, each of which should be called on once a month. A maximum of about fifteen calls can be made in a day, assuming that an adequate job is done at each stop. But these fifteen calls are possible only if the salesman's traveling time is cut to a bare minimum.

Hence, each man is instructed to analyze his territory, determine which are the most important stops to make (those offering greatest potential) and then arrange these accounts geographically, so that no time is wasted, and no important call is omitted. In this way, each month, each week, each day —and each hour—produces maximum sales volume.

This is what I mean by a sales time-table. Remember—things usually happen according to schedule. Without a schedule, things *don't* happen.

So if you increase your selling time—and then increase the productivity of that time—you're bound to step up your sales.

That's the plan.

Chapter 5 in a Nutshell

1. Your time is your money—and it's worth every cent.
2. The clock keeps moving whether **you** do or not. Stay ahead of it.
3. Products can be seasonal. Selling them isn't.
4. Plan your work—work your plan.

Chapter 6

HOW TO OPEN THE DOOR
IN ADVANCE

Getting the Lay of the Land

As every good salesman knows, the opening remarks in a sales presentation are vitally important. What you say during the first few seconds may well decide whether you're going to make the sale or lose it. That's why the entire next Part of the book is devoted to this all-important phase of the sale—the Approach.

But the best super-duper Approach in the world won't do you any good unless you get a chance to use it. First, you have to get in to see the guy.

So there's another step that has to come first. Some people call it the Pre-Approach. I call it simply the Door-Opener.

But, unfortunately, doing it isn't always as easy as saying it. Because opening the prospect's door can often be a long, tough proposition.

And that's why a little preparation—in advance—can pay off handsomely.

The first thing to do is find out something about the prospect—as much as you can. Not just the basic facts we discussed in Chapter 3. They tell you only that he *is* a prospect, and I'm assuming you've already determined that. Now what you want to do is learn some of the specifics about that prospect *as your product or proposition applies to him.*

Of course, if it's an old customer you call on constantly, this is something you already know. Right now we're talking about the new one you've never seen. He doesn't know you, and you can't change that. So you make it your business to "know" him, to whatever extent you can, before you meet him.

What sort of a guy is he? About how old? What's his family like? Any special hobbies?

And how about the company? If you're selling a line of merchandise, what lines does the firm now carry? If you're selling equipment, what are they now using? What are their requirements apt to be? How can you improve service?

Where can you get this information? Well, sometimes you can't. Selling doesn't always follow a strict pattern, and you may have to postpone some of your prospect-education until the actual interview.

But if you keep your eyes and ears open you can learn lots. Read the newspapers. Watch the ads. Check the trade magazines. Talk with other salesmen. Most people like to be helpful.

I remember a sales trip to Hong Kong I made shortly after World War II. I was carrying several good American lines, and I was pretty sure I could find some customers among the various importing firms. But I'd never been within 5000 miles of the place and I had no idea, specifically, whom to call on.

En route, in Manila, I met a salesman who had just returned from Hong Kong. He was a nice fella, too! Because in a half-hour he gave me more information than I could have acquired by myself in a week. I arrived in Hong Kong with a complete list of firms to visit, names of the principals, their various buying habits, even their personal idiosyncrasies.

That advance knowledge was largely responsible for the success of my trip.

Remember, if you find out something about the prospect before you meet him, then you're not meeting a stranger.

And that can make a big difference.

Should You Make an Appointment?

Here again, without knowing specifically what you sell, it's hard to lay down any hard and fast rule. There are several factors involved.

But making a definite appointment to see your prospect, rather than walking in cold, has several advantages, as well as a few disadvantages.

Here are both sides of the coin.

Advantages:

1. Saves time. (And you know how important *that* is!) When you have an appointment, the prospect is pretty sure to be there and see you fairly promptly.

2. Builds prestige. Many businessmen make it a fixed rule never to see salesmen other than by appointment. The appointment makes your visit important.

3. Builds your own self-confidence. With an appointment, you know you'll usually get a fair hearing. This makes you feel better and sell better.

4. Qualifies the prospect. If you got the appointment in the first place, the prospect has, in effect, told you he is interested in what you have to sell.

5. Puts the prospect in a buying mood. When you begin your presentation, the appointment gives you a jumping-off place. You have a head start toward making the sale.

Disadvantages:

There's really only one—but it's a big one. By phoning for an appointment, you give the guy a chance to say no. He might turn you down cold, or he might just put you off—which is just about as bad. If you drop in cold, you might get in. If you ask for an appointment, you might not get it. All is lost.

So those are the angles you have to consider. Essentially, it depends on whether an appointment is apt to be necessary to see the man you want.

It also depends on how skillful you are at making appointments.

And that's why the next part of this chapter is important.

Telephone Techniques

As we've just seen, it's usually a good idea to make an appointment in advance, but a bad idea to phone *without* making one. So it's important to do it right. Here are some tips on how to use the telephone effectively.

1. Plan your pitch. Planning, of course, is always a good idea, but over the phone it's vital. Phone conversations are short. Gestures don't help. Long pauses can be deathly. A single "hem" or "haw" can ruin you. You must know exactly what you want to say, and how you want to say it.

2. Sell the appointment, not the proposition. Some salesmen try to sell the advantages of the product or service over the telephone. This is a common mistake—and a bad one. Naturally, you have to arouse the prospect's interest and make him feel that your story deserves his time. But the time to tell him that story is when you meet him face to face, not before. Right now all you want is the chance to tell it.

3. Don't reveal too much. This is a first cousin to Rule #2. Often the prospect will ask specific questions over the phone —especially regarding price. *Don't answer!* You can't possibly do an adequate selling job, and the prospect can't do an adequate buying job. Naturally, you don't want to insult the man, but you don't want to ruin the sale, either. Do a little fencing if you have to. "Well, naturally, the prices vary depending on the particular model you need, Mr. Jones, and that's why I feel we ought to sit down and discuss it. What day this week would be most convenient for you?"

4. Put a smile in your voice. Remember, this isn't television. The prospect can't see how handsome you are. He doesn't even know what a nice fella you happen to be. Your whole personality is wrapped up in that gadget with the hole in it next to his ear. You don't have to sound like a radio announcer, but you do have to sound pleasant. Because that's all you *can* do —sound.

If you just practice those four rules, your telephone technique will improve, and your appointment-making will be more effective. The telephone can be one of your most valuable sales tools.

You'll find it well worth while to make sure you become an expert at using it.

Putting the Mails to Work

While most sales appointments are logically made over the telephone, you shouldn't forget the wondrous uses of the U. S. Postal System. Actually, there are several ways to use the mails to help open the door in advance.

But, strangely enough, letters are most valuable in two extreme opposite situations: when appointments are easiest to make, and when they're toughest.

A typical example of the first situation is the man who travels a fairly wide area, calling on his customers at infrequent intervals. It isn't hard to get in to see these people. The advance letter is designed simply to let customers know the salesman is coming at a certain time and, perhaps, to whet a few appetites.

In this case, an actual letter is often unnecessary. Usually, a postcard will do the job.

George Abernathy is a top Selling Ace of men's sportswear, covering several Southern states. His firm puts out two lines a year, and holds a sales meeting at the start of each selling season. George brings with him to each meeting a supply of postcards, already typed and addressed to his customers. The card always announces the new line in glowing terms, saying it's the greatest line George has ever seen, and then specifies when George will be in that particular town. The cards are mailed right from the factory for maximum impact. The fact that George wrote them back in his home town in Georgia, long before he saw the merchandise he so passionately described, doesn't destroy their effectiveness at all!

The second situation in which letters are valuable is when you can't get an appointment any other way.

If yours is a high-ticket item—perhaps a special service of some kind—sold to top executives, then it may pay you to write a short note *before* making a telephone call. Like the telephone conversation, the letter shouldn't be too revealing. It should simply announce the fact that you have something highly important to present, and that you will phone for an appointment at the prospect's convenience.

But be sure to specify when you will call—and then make the phone call at that exact time. It's hard for the prospect to turn down an approach like that.

Letters, like phone calls, pave the way for a more successful sales presentation—with one difference. He can't say no to a sheet of paper!

The Traveling Salesman Gambit

As indicated in the last few pages, the salesman who travels has several advantages. Because he's from out of town, buyers will usually see him at *his* convenience. If he's only in town for this week, no one will ask him to come back *next* week. They may not buy, but at least they'll give him a break and let him tell his story.

Which brings up one of my favorite appointment-making techniques. I've seen it work time after time, in all lines of business. I've never seen it fail. *Never.*

It's simply this: Whatever you sell, wherever you sell, become a traveling salesman! Even if you never move out of a square-mile area, become a traveling salesman!

Now, I don't mean that quite literally. What I *do* mean is that you'll be more successful at making appointments if you limit the time you have available. Don't make appointments *entirely* at the other fellow's convenience. Let him know that you *can't* see him next month. For whatever reason, it's got to be *now.*

And if you can make this an actual fact by doing some traveling, so much the better.

When I was a manufacturer's representative in Hawaii, the huge majority of our volume came from the city of Honolulu, where we had our showroom. And, of course, we had the same problem common to all hometown salesmen—the buyers always wanted to see us *next* week.

So I bought an airplane and scheduled regular trips to the other islands. We never expected to get very much business from these outlying areas, although, as a matter of fact, we did.

But the best part was that we *traveled*. From that moment on, *we* had the control. We could say—with complete honesty: "Sorry, Mr. Jones, but *next* week we'll be in Kaunakakai!" That stopped 'em!

Chapter 6 in a Nutshell

1. Like the doctor: to solve problems, you have to know what the problems are.
2. The only disadvantage to an appointment is if you fail to make it.
3. The telephone is a wonderful instrument. Learn to play it.
4. A card isn't hard, but a letter is better.
5. Away from home the prophet is never without honor, the salesman never without appointments.

Chapter 7

WINNING THE BATTLE
OF THE OUTSIDE OFFICE

How to Get By the Outer Guard

If you follow the suggestions covered in Chapter 6, you'll make the job of getting in to see your prospect a lot easier. The door will already be open—part way, at least.

But the outside office can still be quite a battleground. Here are some tips to help you win the fight.

And, of course, if you *haven't* made an appointment in advance, that sentry behind the receptionist's desk is apt to be a formidable obstacle.

But, let's face it, she's got a job to do, too. That job, very simply, is to *screen* everybody who wants in. And that's a good thing. Because if she let in *every* character who wanted to sell the boss something, he'd never have time to see *you!*

So you're really on her side. You don't *want* her to be too easy. You just want her to make an exception in *your* case.

And the only way to do that, obviously, is to give her reason to believe that your visit is important to the company. If she feels that the boss *ought* to see you, and conveys that to the other side of the wall, you've usually got it made.

This means, of course, that you have to do some selling on the receptionist, and everything in this book applies here just the same as it does on the inside.

First of all, you have to act as if you expect to get in. Don't shuffle nervously up to the gal and mumble something about, "I'd like to—er—see somebody about typewriters."

Walk up to her like a man! Smile (of course) and make a straightforward statement like: "Hello, I'm Joe Doakes. I'd like to see Mr. Jones for a few minutes about cutting costs in the office."

When she asks whether you have an appointment, you simply say (assuming you don't): "No, as a matter of fact, he isn't expecting me. But in ten minutes I think I can help save this company a lot of money—and make your own work a lot easier, too!"

Again, it's impossible for me to be specific here. Each situation is different.

But the essential principle remains the same. Be natural, be human, be a nice guy—but make it plain that you're there on business. You didn't come just to leave a calling card.

Talking about business cards, opinion varies greatly as to their value. Some salesmen look upon cards as nothing more than loose paper dog-tags. Others don't even carry them. But I know at least one Selling Ace, Ed Long of the Sales Promotion Essentials Corporation, who uses his business card as a passport into New York's innermost inner sanctums.

Here's how he does it.

Stepping up to the receptionist (and before the gal has a chance to tell him the boss is busy) Ed pencils a personal note on the back of his card, and asks her to take it inside. Letters can be pigeonholed and phone calls can be sidetracked. But here's a direct, on-the-spot, intra-office memo that can hardly miss its target.

Now, of course, when the boss gets the note, he can always send back word for Ed to go jump in a lake. But that seldom happens. By using his business card as a personal envoy, announcing his visit directly to the head man—not just to the receptionist—Ed makes that visit important enough to get the time he wants with the man he's there to see.

The card gets in. And so, usually, does Ed Long.

There's one thing to watch out for, however. Don't try to trick your way in. For two reasons. First, it won't work. Second,

if it does get you in, you'll be on your way out just as quick.
And you won't get back.

You'll get in if you deserve to—honestly.

And That Deathly Inner Guard

This chapter is supposed to confine itself to what happens
on the outside—in the waiting room. Perhaps we shouldn't be
talking here about anything that goes on once you're admitted
to the inner sanctum.

But sometimes—especially in big companies—you find yourself in a sort of "middle" sanctum. And trying to sell there is
just as hopeless as pitching your deal at the receptionist.

This is when that nice fellow greets you in his cell, offers
you a chair, and listens politely—but he has no authority to
buy. We touched on this in Chapter 3. Remember? You *must*
tell your story to the man who can buy.

Of course, if you had checked first to find out who *is* your
real prospect, you wouldn't find yourself in this spot. You just
wouldn't go in to see anyone else.

But occasionally you can't help yourself. You're facing the
wrong guy, he's waiting to hear the story. What do you do?

Answer: You don't tell it to him! Except under *very* special
circumstances. Because, as I've said, it would be a waste of
time.

Naturally, you don't want to insult the man. Even though
he can't O.K. the deal, he *can* queer it.

Your best bet is to try to arrange a date with him *and* the
boss. If you can't get together with both of them right then
and there, set up another appointment. An approach like this
usually solves the problem: "Mr. Jones, I know you have a
lot of influence here, but if Mr. Smith is going to have to O.K.
the final decision, let's *all* get together so that *both* of you can
hear the story first-hand."

The important thing, of course, is to learn the score and get
this point across as *quickly* as possible. You've wasted enough
time already.

Wait Time Needn't Be Waste Time

Back in Chapter 5 we covered the tremendous value of your time.

Unfortunately—but unavoidably—most salesmen spend many hours every week waiting to see people. Now, briefly, let's discuss exactly what you do during those precious hours.

Because, while this time can't pay off in signed orders, it doesn't have to go as a complete waste.

First, you can check up on yourself. Are your samples, selling material, etc. in good order? Can you think of any additional selling points to include in your presentation? What objections can you anticipate?

Second, you can check up on the prospect. Can you get any extra help from the receptionist? Are any of the company's products, advertisements, literature, etc., on display? What can you learn from them? How about the office layout itself? Does that give you any clues that will help you plan your presentation?

In a salesman's Utopia, waiting time would be eliminated. When you find it, let me know. Until then, let's *use* that time the best way we know how.

Always Use a Sales Warm-Up

So far, we've covered just about everything that happens —or *should* happen—before the actual sale begins. Because these are the techniques that top salesmen use to Start with a Spade. Now the stage is set and the curtain is going up.

But between the time that the gal issues that welcome proclamation, "Mr. Soandso will see you now," and the moment you shake hands with Mr. Prospect, there is just *one* more thing you can do to boost your chances. Even this brief interlude can be important.

Use a sales warm-up! Just a 10-second personal pep talk.

Howard Thurston, the famous magician, used to do this every evening just before curtain time. He'd jump up and down in the wings and say, "I love my audience! I love my audience!"

Sound corny? Sure! But it worked.

Some salesmen like to take a few deep breaths. Others straighten their ties. Or maybe you'd prefer just to think about that TV set you figure on winning in the contest.

Actually, it makes little difference. *What* you do is not important. Whatever thought or action will put you in the best selling frame of mind—that's the thing to use. You don't even have to tell anybody about it! As long as it helps *you*, that's all that counts.

O.K.? Ready?

Good! Now get in there and *sell!*

Chapter 7 in a Nutshell

1. Get the receptionist to help you out—and help you in.
2. Don't pitch unless you have the right catcher.
3. Don't play the waiting game—work at it.
4. Always use a sales warm-up—and you'll never go in cold.

PART II

A ♥

Selling Ace #2
IN EVERY APPROACH

HIT 'EM IN THE
HEART

♥ A

Chapter 8

A LOOK INSIDE THE CUSTOMER

Buyers Are People

Let me ask you a question. How many different prospects do you call on each year? What would *you* say? 100? 500? 1000?

Well, I'll tell you a secret—if you don't already know it. You don't call on *any* different prospects! Honestly, for the most part, they're all the same.

Sure, they *look* different. They come in various sizes, ages and shapes. Each has his own distinctive personality. And probably every single one of 'em will tell you he *is* different from all the rest.

But don't you believe it! It just isn't so. Because buyers are all *people*—and people are all pretty much alike.

I remember when I first decided to leave my home town of Honolulu, Hawaii, and strike out for New York. My friends told me I'd hate the Mainland. I was used to the easy-going ways of the tropics, they said. I'd never be able to take the hustle-bustle and razzle-dazzle of the Big City.

But it didn't work out that way. Folks are folks wherever you go.

And that goes double for *customers*. Because when people are buying something, there's a set pattern they usually follow. They buy for the same reasons.

There are exceptions, of course. The same man, in fact,

may have different motives for buying various products. A purchasing agent, for instance, buys equipment for his firm for one reason; he'll buy his family a swimming pool for quite another.

But here you're not especially interested in various products. You care about the one particular type of product or service you sell. The heck with the rest!

So in this Part we'll analyze *why* people buy, why they buy *your product*, and how you can *capitalize* on these universal buying instincts and make them pay off.

The First Person Principle

O.K. People are all pretty much alike, and everybody buys your product or service for essentially the same reasons.

But there's one main point to remember:

Everybody's interested in himself. His benefit. *His* satisfaction. *His* profit. All any customer really wants to know is: *"What's in it for me?"*

This is probably the most important rule in selling. I call it The First Person Principle. Here's what it means.

According to the grammar books, "I" is the pronoun of the *first person.* As far as *I* am concerned, *I* am the person of first importance. That's not being selfish or conceited. It's just the way things are. We all feel the same way.

Back in grade school, my English teacher once asked the class: "If you and another boy were crossing a street, and a car suddenly came speeding toward you, whose life would you try to save?"

Some kid in the back of the room, who had just taken his Scout oath, piped up, "The other guy's."

But the rest of us agreed we'd think of *ourselves* first. Everybody does.

Including your customer!

Nobody *ever* gives you an order to please *you.* Or your boss. Or your company. He buys because he believes it's a good deal for *him.*

Whatever you sell, whatever features it offers, you have to talk *in terms of the benefit to your customer*.

Not What It Is—What It Will DO

If the customer is interested in himself—not you or your product—obviously he's interested in what his purchase will *do* for him.

So don't get *too* wrapped up in your own product knowledge. In Part I we talked about the importance of being an expert on whatever you sell. That's true. *You* have to know everything there is to know about it. But your customer doesn't! He may not want to. If he asks a question, you've got to be ready to answer it. But usually the buyer doesn't care exactly how it's made, what goes into it or what makes it tick. All he *really* wants to know is what it will *do*.

The Rubber and Asbestos Corporation of Bloomfield, New Jersey, manufactures various kinds of adhesives for industrial use. Inasmuch as their products are highly technical, most of their salesmen are also chemical engineers. But among the *top producers,* several of the men have had no real training in chemistry at all.

How come? The Selling Aces don't sell the product—they sell the *results.*

You've heard the old gag about why firemen wear red suspenders. The answer is simple. Why? To keep their pants up! That's all.

I happen to smoke a pipe. Like all pipe-smokers, I use a lot of matches. I buy 'em by the carton, stuff my pockets every morning, grab a couple of packs during lunch at the restaurant, and raid my secretary's desk for more almost every afternoon.

Yet I've never wanted a match in my life. All I've ever wanted was to *light my pipe!*

Back in Hawaii, a friend of mine was purchasing agent for a large sugar plantation. He was a real old-timer, of Japanese descent, with little formal education. But he sure knew the sugar business!

A manufacturer of bolo knives, who happened to be vacationing in the Islands, took time off from the beach long enough to visit my friend.

As head of the firm, this executive knew every phase of his product's manufacture. He told the purchasing agent exactly how his bolo knives were made. He explained how the blade was solidly embedded in the handle, how the precise curvature of the blade was scientifically designed, and how the handle was treated with an improved new formula of lacquer.

He forgot just one thing, the *only* thing my friend really wanted to know. After a 20-minute sales talk, the old Japanese said: "That all sounds pretty good. But tell me: *How will it cut sugar?*"

So remember. All the features of your product that are so important to *you* may not mean a thing to your customer. What *he* wants to know is: *"What will it do for me?"*

People Buy Through the Heart

Here's another vital selling rule:

People don't buy what they *think* they *need*—they buy what they *feel* they *want*. They buy through the *heart*.

Take yourself as an example.

How about the house you live in? Did you take it because of the exact size and shape of the rooms? Or, when you signed the papers, were you thinking instead about the happiness you and your family could enjoy?

Or what about your favorite suit? Did you really care whether it had two buttons or three? Or, as you stood in front of the mirror, were you simply trying to decide whether it made you look good? (Notice I didn't ask you how the *suit* looked. That's not important. It's how the suit made *you* look that mattered.)

I'll bet the same goes for everything you own. You bought through the *heart*.

Your customers do, too! If you want to sell 'em, you have to *Hit 'Em in the Heart*.

You see another good example of this every time you visit your corner newsstand.

Take a look at the magazine display. There may be hundreds of different publications, covering everything from astronautics to zoology. Obviously, some people are interested in every one of these subjects. They're important *things*.

But the magazines that enjoy the widest circulation, invariably, are the ones about *people*. Why? Because they *Hit 'Em in the Heart*.

Charles Lindbergh was probably the greatest American hero of the century. Why? Not just because he flew the Atlantic. The U. S. Navy did it in 1919. So did a couple of Englishmen. An Army plane made it all the way around the world in 1924. And prior to Lindbergh's flight in 1927, literally dozens of people had crossed the Atlantic by dirigible. None of these exploits attracted much attention, even at the time.

But Lindbergh was something different! He was young, good looking, hard working and unassuming—the typical All-American boy in the first chapter of the typical All-American story.

The whole world bought Lindbergh because he *Hit 'Em in the Heart*.

So, right now, if you're selling typewriters, STOP—sell attention-getting letters.

If you're selling medical equipment, STOP—sell patient comfort.

If you're selling breakfast cereal, STOP—sell healthy, happy youngsters.

Because people buy through the *heart*. It's the only way to sell 'em.

Chapter 8 in a Nutshell

1. Buyers are all people, and people are all pretty much the same.
2. Everybody's interested in himself. All the buyer wants to know is: "What's in it for me?"
3. Don't tell 'em what it is—tell 'em what it will do.
4. Everybody buys through the heart. You have to sell 'em the same way.

Chapter 9

THE H-E-A-R-T FORMULA

Having taken a general look inside the customer, now let's get more specific.

Because you can't Hit 'Em in the Heart unless you know what people really want when they buy your product.

The basic appeals that make people buy are called Heart-Appeals. Let's see what they are.

Here's the formula:

H-ealth
E-njoyment
A-chievement
R-omance
T-reasure

Health

The first law of nature is self-preservation. All over the world, millions and millions of people are working just to stay alive. The gourmet who won't touch anything less than filet mignon in his favorite restaurant back home, will eat the bark off trees when he becomes lost in the jungle. Condemned prisoners always make their last-minute appeals, hoping they'll be allowed to live a little longer in prison. And police records are full of cases in which people have tied heavy weights to their clothing before jumping into a river, only to struggle loose to keep from drowning!

Above everything else, human beings want to *live*.

But, for most of us, life means little without good *health*. The two go hand in hand.

That's why so much of today's great medical research is aimed not just at saving lives, but at preventing illness. It's also why accident and health insurance is sold almost as widely today as life insurance. And it's why the patent medicines are a multi-million dollar industry.

Minute-Maid Fresh Frozen Orange Juice advertises: "When they want more, there's more *health* to pour."

Among drinkers of other beverages, "To your *health!*" is the favorite toast in almost every language.

Because *health*—along with self-preservation—is what everyone wants more than anything else in the world.

Enjoyment

But we Americans want not only life—and not only a healthy life—we want a *good* life. We want *enjoyment*. It's second on the list of basic buying appeals.

The Milton Bradley Company of Springfield, Massachusetts, manufactures children's games. One of their Selling Aces once told me he'd tried every approach he could think of. He used to emphasize the educational value of his products. He'd point out how cleverly they were designed, and how easy they were to play. But the only factor that counted, he told me, was whether they were *fun*.

And this applies not only to games. *Enjoyment* is a basic human want. You can use it to sell almost anything.

Go through the pages of any leading national magazine. Of all the ads—for all kinds of products—about half of them (including most of the good ones) show people using the product and having *fun*.

A good example is cigarette advertising, which has recently undergone an almost total revolution.

For years the various brands competed largely on the basis of quality of manufacture. The ads spoke of tobacco ingredients, blends and secret processes. Then, for a while, the "medical claims" campaigns were prominent. (The health appeal.)

But now most of the ads claim just one thing: the cigarette is *fun* to smoke. And cigarettes are selling faster than ever. Because *enjoyment* is what folks are looking for when they light up.

The tremendous do-it-yourself boom originally came about primarily because most people couldn't afford to hire outside help. Many homeowners found that the carpenters, plumbers and electricians were making more money than *they* were! But today millions of folks in top income brackets are "doing-it-themselves" too. Why? Because it gives them *enjoyment*.

Every year folks have more leisure time. They want to *enjoy* it.

Achievement

This is one of the most important of all buying appeals—and yet one that's most often neglected by salesmen.

Everybody wants to *be* somebody. Years ago almost every father wanted his son to grow up and become President of the United States. Perhaps that job is not coveted by quite so many people today. But certainly *everyone* wants to get ahead, especially in the eyes of other people. Everyone wants to "keep up with the Joneses."

So this is another appeal you can apply to almost any sales talk.

It's especially important when calling on business firms—and this is when most salesmen forget to use it.

Because *companies* never buy anything. Some *person within* the company has to make the decision, and some *person within* the company has to sign the check. Remember? Buyers are *people*. Even committees are made up of *people*.

Of course, this becomes obvious when you're talking to the small one-man organization, or even the owner of a medium-sized family-owned corporation. In these situations there's only one boss. You know it and he knows it. So you naturally talk to him as an individual. You use the achievement appeal, along with any others that apply, as a matter of course.

But in a large corporation, people tend to hide their own individuality. They wave the company flag, speak with an editorial "we" and want you to believe their only love is for dear old Amalgamated Widgets.

Now, I think good company morale is a wonderful thing. I'm all for it. But when you're out selling, don't fall for this flag-waving routine completely.

Because the man you're talking to is still an *individual*. He's a lot more concerned with his *own* welfare than he is with his firm's. His job, his future, his success—they all come first. That, you remember, is The First Person Principle.

So no matter how fancy the office or how large the desk, remember that the fellow on the other side of it is interested mainly in *himself*, his own *achievement*. If you can show him how your proposition will put a feather in *his* cap, you've hit him in the heart.

Because everybody wants *achievement*.

As a matter of fact, this is one reason why people go to the movies. Of course, the more obvious reason is because they *enjoy* movies. (There's that enjoyment again.)

But Hollywood uses the achievement appeal, too. Because when the hero of the piece finally gets the girl in the last scene, every guy in the audience sees *himself* getting the girl. The same girl! Meanwhile, in the next seat, his wife is imagining *herself* getting that gorgeous hunk of man on the screen!

As Schlitz Beer, another of our clients, says in the ads: "How American it is to want something better!"

Romance

Here, as we all know, is one of the most basic appeals of all. Ever since Eve lured Adam, *romance* has been one of the world's great driving forces.

And here again, we have an appeal that can be applied to almost any product.

Just one word of caution. Sex, to be effective as a buying appeal, must be *subtle*. Looking once more at advertising, a lot of it is overdone in this direction. If romance actually has no connection with your product, you'd better leave this one out.

But it's amazing how many products *can* be sold successfully with a strong appeal to romance.

An obvious example is the cosmetics industry. In working with Elizabeth Arden sales demonstrators, I've noticed they never sell what's in the jar. They sell what happens *after* the woman puts the stuff on her face! Because every woman longs to be beautiful—not to other women, but to men!

Dancing lessons are sold on this same basis. How many folks study ballet or tap dancing? Only a few—the ones who want to learn how to *dance*, for the sake of dancing. Yet millions every year visit the Arthur Murray studios. Why? Because Arthur Murray offers more than dancing lessons—he sells *romance*.

There are many other products that fit into the romance category, too, perhaps less obviously.

The fabulous boom in the travel business has been spurred on by this same appeal. Every season of the year, married couples sail away by the boat-load and take off by the plane-load, all looking for a second honeymoon—while an equal number of *un*marrieds travel in the hopes of latching on to a first! And the most popular resorts are always the spots that are *romantic*.

Even some towel and sheet manufacturers sell their goods the same way, only in reverse. A top executive at Fieldcrest Mills told me recently about a survey they had taken. It showed that businessmen who travel enjoy the clean sheets offered by every hotel, and miss them when they return home. So Fieldcrest began a new campaign. With nice clean sheets and color-coordinated towels and pillow cases, they said, you put romance back in the *home!*

No doubt about it. Romance is a strong appeal. If you can fit it to your product, don't fail to take advantage of it.

Treasure

Finally, the appeal of *money*. I doubt if I'll have to convince you about this one.

Because if the love of money is the root of all evil, most of us have some awful wicked customers!

Actually, many salesmen stress this appeal *too* strongly. Because a low price—by itself—never sells anything. Most people realize they can't get something for nothing. A bargain isn't a bargain unless it gives folks what they want. You have to sell the proposition *first*.

Still, *after* you've got the customer sold, the idea of saving money has obvious appeal.

With businessmen, of course, *profit* is the strongest possible appeal in most cases. (Although, as we saw earlier, it isn't the *only* appeal.) Show a man how he can *make money* with your product or service, and you've usually got yourself a deal.

So if you sell to business, let me say again: don't get too involved with discussions about the *product*. If it makes money, it's good; if it doesn't, it's bad.

One of my good friends is Melvin P. Vaught, Vice-President of the J. J. Newberry Company, the variety department store chain. They operate about 500 stores from coast to coast, and their business growth in recent years has been phenomenal.

The other day Mel was telling me one of the secrets of their success. "Our buyers have strict instructions *not* to buy according to their own personal tastes," he said. "We tell them not to buy what *they* like—buy what will *sell* at a *profit*."

So if your merchandise is bought for resale, keep that in mind.

Show the buyer how *he* can sell your goods profitably and *you'll* sell 'em! Don't worry too much about moving your items *into* his place of business. Think about moving them *out!* Why? Because that's what *he's* thinking about.

If you sell businessmen some product or service for their own use, the problem is somewhat different. But the principle is the same.

Possibly your product doesn't exactly *make* money for the customer. Maybe it *saves* money. Often that's even more important.

Right now the private airplane industry is enjoying its biggest boom since Wilbur and Orville took off at Kitty Hawk. Even with the wonders of jet airline travel, more and more business firms are buying their own light aircraft.

Much of this boom is due to the successful marketing methods of the Cessna Aircraft Company, of Wichita, Kansas. My friend Frank Martin, Sales Manager, told me that they did it largely by going after the companies already spending money on travel, and showing them how to *cut costs* with a Cessna.

The whole point is this: Mis-used, *money* alone doesn't sell. But properly handled, *treasure* can be your strongest Heart-Appeal of all.

Chapter 9 in a Nutshell

This is the formula by which people buy:

1. **H-EALTH:** Without life there's nothing. Without health there's not much more.
2. **E-NJOYMENT:** After life and health, happiness comes next as the basic human want.
3. **A-CHIEVEMENT:** Everybody wants to be somebody, and to let other folks know it.
4. **R-OMANCE:** Love makes the world go 'round—and your sales go up.
5. **T-REASURE:** Whether you're rich or poor, it's nice to have money.

Therefore, it's the formula by which you must sell.

Chapter 10

FITTING THE FORMULA TO YOUR OWN PRODUCT

Now comes the really important part of the whole H-E-A-R-T Formula—applying it to your own product or service.

Here is how you can get immediate favorable attention from every prospect you call on—by Hitting 'Em in the Heart.

Make Up a Heart-Appeal Check List

Let's get down to specifics.

You have a product, or line of products, or service to sell. You've already Started with a Spade—you know your product inside out, you know your competition, you know your prospects, and you know where to find them.

You also know the H-E-A-R-T Formula, which tells you why people buy.

Now all you have to do is fit the formula to your own product—pick out the specific Heart-Appeals to use in your own selling.

The best way to do this is to make up a Heart-Appeal Check List.

Of course, *I* don't have the facts about *your* product. You do. So all I can do is tell you how to go about it—you'll have to do the rest.

On the next page is a sample of the Heart-Appeal Check

List that we use in our Sales Workshops around the country. You can simply fill it in, right in the book—or, better yet, make a copy on regular letter paper, which you can put in your notebook or sales manual.

That way, you'll always have it with you, and it may remind you to *use* your Heart-Appeals on every call. They're no good unless you put them to work.

Heart-Appeal Check List for Ford Cars

Right now you want to make up your own Heart-Appeal Check List. But just to help show you how to do it, let's take an example.

One of our clients is the Ford Motor Company. (For their Latin American dealers, in fact, Ford uses the formula in Spanish!) So let's find out how the formula applies to a Ford automobile.

Then I think you'll see how to do the same for your own product.

Health

Does this apply to a Ford? Admittedly, self-preservation and health are not primary reasons for buying a Ford. Let's face it. Thousands of people are killed in automobiles every year. If anyone wanted to avoid driving hazards completely they'd stay home!

But today a car is almost a necessity. People do drive. So they want their car to be as safe as possible. There's a clue! *Safety!*

So in the Heart column we put Ford's Lifeguard Design, Deep-Center Steering Wheel, and Safety-Swivel Rearview Mirror. Expressed in terms of *safety*, these are definitely Heart-Appeals.

What are the health appeals in *your* product? Write 'em down.

Buyers Are All People—and All People Buy Through the Heart. You Have to Sell 'Em the Same Way.

YOUR NAME _____

PRODUCT OR SERVICE YOU SELL _____

THE H-E-A-R-T FORMULA Basic Buying Instincts	HOW DOES YOUR PRODUCT FIT THE FORMULA? List Here All the Specific Appeals for Your Product that Satisfy Each Instinct
H EALTH	
E NJOYMENT	
A CHIEVEMENT	
R OMANCE	
T REASURE	

IN EVERY APPROACH, HIT 'EM IN THE HEART!

Enjoyment

Here's a natural. Any car—new or used—provides transportation. But surveys show that many folks choose a new Ford because they find it *fun to drive*.

So among our enjoyment appeals we can list Ford's Thunderbird Power, driving ease, and lively performance.

Do folks get fun out of using *your* product? How? Write it down.

Achievement

This is really the main underlying reason why most people buy a new car. Because the fellow who bought, say, three years ago doesn't really *need* a new car. The one he's got has plenty of miles left in it.

But a new automobile means *prestige*. It's probably the number one symbol of status in America.

So here we talk about Thunderbird Styling, Luxury Lounge interiors, and the Brussels World's Fair Gold Medal Award.

What achievement appeals can you find for *your* product? List them.

Romance

We've covered most of the main Ford buying appeals. Now let's see if romance fits in. At first glance it doesn't. But sometimes the best Heart-Appeals are the ones you have to hunt for.

For the bachelor, Ford promises romance in a big way. Gals are pretty choosy these days. They prefer to date the fellow who takes 'em out in style. A new car certainly helps.

So, again, all the styling features play an important role.

Even for the married man, romance comes into the Ford story. The guy who puts a beautiful new car under the Christmas tree is going to rate mighty high with his wife!

Does romance fit into *your* sales talk? If not, leave it out.

But if you *can* find some valid romance appeals, latch on to 'em. They belong in your list.

Treasure

Applied to an automobile, this means *economy*, and it's a vitally important appeal for anyone.

Because any new car represents a major investment. A man wants to know that he's making a *wise* investment, and that his investment will be *protected*.

So Ford's low original price, high gasoline mileage, and extra trade-in value, all score as major Heart-Appeals in the treasure column.

Does *your* product help folks save money? How? Or does it *make* money? Be sure to include these appeals in *your* Heart-Appeal Check List.

Checking the Check List

Now that you've got your Heart-Appeal Check List made up, you're ready to go out and use it to make more sales and more money. That's what it's for.

But wait!

If you want your Heart-Appeals to really pay off, there are three things to watch for. They're simple—but important.

Here they are:

1. *Exclusive Appeals are Best.* In Part I we talked about the importance of knowing your competitor's product, as well as your own. Why? Because then you can emphasize the *exclusive* Heart-Appeals that are yours alone.

Heart-Appeals score best when they are available *only from you.*

So in checking your Heart-Appeal Check List, make sure you emphasize the *exclusive* appeals. If you talk about something *everybody* offers, why should the prospect buy from *you?*

When Milton Reynolds first came out with his ball-point pen after World War II, it was the *only* pen that could write for weeks without refilling. When Reynolds advertised it as the modern pen for successful men, he was using an *exclusive* achievement appeal, and millions were sold at $15. Today you can buy several far superior pens at less than $2. Why? Because the basic appeal is no longer *exclusive*.

Right now the Polaroid Land Camera sells successfully at a price far above that of many other popular cameras. Why? Because Polaroid can claim it's the *only* camera that develops fine pictures right on the spot. That's an *exclusive* appeal aimed at enjoyment.

Raleigh is still the only leading brand of cigarettes that offers premium coupons with every pack. Raleighs are sold with an *exclusive* treasure appeal. As we discussed earlier, money is not always the prime factor, which is probably why Raleigh is not the largest selling brand. But it's still their best *exclusive* Heart-Appeal.

So right now go over your Heart-Appeal Check List, and underline the appeals that are *exclusive*. They're the ones that will do you the most good.

Here's one place you can cheat a little. Because often you can get by with a Heart-Appeal that may *not* be exclusive, so long as your customer *thinks* it is.

Millions of people buy Gleem Toothpaste, for instance, because it has GL-70. Pepsodent has for years advertised its special Irium. Do you know what these mysterious ingredients are? I don't.

This modern business phenomenon was pointed up recently in a cartoon in one of the advertising trade publications.

The scene was the head office of a large corporation, apparently a manufacturer of drug products. The advertising agency was making a presentation. There were magazine layouts, posters, counter cards, window streamers and billboards. All featured a smiling face and a big, bold headline proclaiming, "Now with QX-93!"

The boss had his mouth open, and the caption read: "That's great, Boys, but *whatinhell is QX-93?*"

So no matter what you sell, no matter how competitive your

industry, you can always find *some* Heart-Appeal that *sounds* exclusive, at least.

But keep checking for the appeals that *are* exclusive.

Exclusive Heart-Appeals are always best.

2. *You Need Facts, Too.* Your Heart-Appeals are aimed mainly at getting favorable attention. They hold out the "pot of gold at the end of the rainbow" and offer the "castles in Spain" that everybody wants. Without them you'll never succeed as a Selling Ace. I mean *really* succeed, the way you should.

But for every Heart-Appeal, you must have *facts* to back it up. You can't promise anything you can't deliver.

So take another look at your Heart-Appeal Check List, and make sure there's a *reason behind* every appeal you offer. They have to be *guaranteed*.

During the hectic years immediately following World War II, the Tucker automobile was heralded as a modern automotive miracle. With a gigantic publicity campaign, Tucker announced that his car would revolutionize the industry. What happened? Tucker was hauled into court, and the trusting souls who invested in his venture lost their shirts. *He couldn't deliver.*

Back in Honolulu there was a wonderful character named Jimmy Walker (no relation to New York's erstwhile mayor). Jimmy was in the night club business, and he was a great promoter.

First he opened a glamorous spot, with a revolving bar, called La Hula Rumba. It went broke. Then, with a new backer, he started an intimate little bottle club named Gentleman Jim's—invitation by card only. It closed within a few months. Another place, the Lamp Post, met a similar fate. Jimmy was involved in a whole succession of brilliant restaurant ideas, but they all failed.

Jimmy's ventures were all loaded with Heart-Appeals. Being a sincere guy at heart, he tried to give people what they wanted. *But he just couldn't deliver.*

Throughout the country there are thousands of one-shot

salesmen who promise anything to make a sale, without having the stuff to back it up. Maybe they're making out OK—today. But, believe me, there's no future to this sort of selling.

So Heart-Appeals—by themselves—are not enough. You have to be able to *deliver*.

And to do that, you have to be able to *prove* what you say. Make sure you back up your Heart-Appeals with *facts*.

3. *The Final Test*. Now that you've made up your Heart-Appeal Check List—and checked it—you're all set to put it to work. You should be rarin' to go!

There's just one final point.

No matter how thoughtfully you've made it up, no matter how carefully you've checked it, it still needs someone else's stamp of approval—the customer's!

The one final test for every appeal is: Did it Hit 'Em in the Heart and help make 'em buy?

Your Heart-Appeal Check List is actually never finished. As you use it, you'll invariably find that some appeals don't quite hit the mark. You'll discover others that pay off better. Don't be afraid to make changes.

But when you've got it working, stick to it! It's worth its weight in gold.

Chapter 10 in a Nutshell

1. Make up a Heart-Appeal Check List to fit your own product or service.
2. Analyze your product—include as many different appeals as you can.
3. Try to use Heart-Appeals that are **exclusive**.
4. Back 'em up with **facts**—be sure you can deliver the goods.
5. Finally—get the **customer's** stamp of approval.

Chapter 11

HOW TO PUT THE
FORMULA TO WORK

Plan Your Opening Gambit

The only way to make successful approaches consistently
is to plan them. That, of course, is the main reason for making
up a Heart-Appeal Check List in the first place.

Because, while Heart-Appeals can work wonders for you
throughout the sale, they're especially important in your approach.

But you've got to decide *how* you're going to use them—
exactly what you're going to say.

Some salesmen disagree with this. They like to "play it by
ear." But you can't play a song by ear unless you *know* it.
Someone had to *write* it first. And that's why Selling Aces
never call on a prospect without planning the approach in
advance.

In this sense, selling is a lot like playing chess.

You can never tell for sure how the game will develop in
its later stages. That's why you need all that product information, all those Heart-Appeals, and—as we'll see later—all the
answers to possible objections.

But you *can* tell how the game is going to *start*. Because
you start it!

And that's why experienced chess players have a few favorite "opening gambits" that always get the game started the way they want.

You must do the same.

3 Sure-Fire Starters

The exact phrasing of your opening gambit may depend on several unknown factors—unknown, that is, to me. Based on the particular circumstances surrounding a specific call, or the source of the lead, or even your own personality, you may decide to launch any given sale in a certain way. That's fine.

But a few "stock" openers are necessary, too.

Here are three that are *guaranteed* to get *any* sale off to a good start. Maybe not *every* time, but darn near it. And the beauty of them is that they'll fit *any* product, *any* prospect, *any* Heart-Appeal.

Here they are:

> 1. "How would you like to . . ."
> 2. "I've got an idea that will . . ."
> 3. "I think I can help you . . ."

As I said, they'll work for any product—including yours. But just as an example, let's take life insurance.

One of our clients—and a very real friend—is Charlie Barton, President of the C. B. Knight Agency in New York, the largest life insurance agency in America. Of all the Heart-Appeals for insurance, Charlie tells me that *achievement* is one of the most potent. With insurance, for instance, any man can guarantee a college education for his children. That's a real Heart-Appeal!

Let's see how this works with my three favorite stock openers, and how those three openers work for the insurance Selling Ace.

1. *"How would you like to guarantee a college education for your children?"*

Here, the Heart-Appeal is expressed as a simple, straightforward question. There's no mincing of words. No "ifs" or "buts". And the further advantage of this particular gambit is that it almost *forces* the prospect to say: "Yes, I'd like that fine!" Right away, you have the prospect agreeing with you. You're off to a flying start.

2. *"I've got an idea that will guarantee a college education for your children."*

This is just a little softer. It doesn't demand an affirmative answer quite so insistently. But it has tremendous power—all wrapped up in the word "idea". Just as I'm writing this, one of the world's largest advertising agencies, Young and Rubicam, is running a series of ads for its own services, aimed at top companies. The headline states: "People buy *ideas*." And how true that is! Tell a man you have an *idea* that will accomplish something he wants done, and he'll want to hear more.

3. *"I think I can help you guarantee a college education for your children."*

This is the softest sell of the bunch, yet in several ways the most effective. The word "think" is decidedly not negative, but it's not *too* positive. It indicates that you just might be wrong about the whole thing—but you probably aren't. The word "help" always scores, because it shows you're interested in the other fellow—and, of course, as we pointed out in Chapter 8, that's exactly what *he's* interested in, himself. So, again, you get started on the right track.

Notice, in all three of these examples, the Heart-Appeal remained precisely the same. The only change was in the introductory phrase.

So whatever you sell—and whomever you sell—try these three openers.

They're sure-fire.

Selling with Reverse English

So far we've been talking about the things that people want.

Now let's consider the things people *don't* want. Because they're important, too.

What *don't* people want? That's easy. The exact opposites of the things they *do* want!

Actually, every one of the Heart-Appeals can be reversed

and used in a sort of "double-negative" approach, and sometimes this is even more effective.

Take Health. In China, they say, you don't go to a doctor to cure you and make you well—you pay him to keep you from getting sick! Speaking of insurance again, many folks buy not because of the benefits they'll get, but because of the hardships they'll *avoid*.

The same way with Enjoyment. Some people go out at night for excitement—others do it to *avoid* the boredom of staying home.

How about Achievement? Look at the ads for correspondence schools. Some hold out the promise of business advancement, but the Alexander Hamilton Institute, one of the very finest, has for years aimed its appeal at the men who want to *avoid* being failures.

Or Romance. The gals who read the cosmetics ads usually get a hint of what wonders can be in store if they do use the stuff, but Listerine tells 'em frankly what will happen if they *don't!*

And finally, that old Treasure appeal. Benjamin Franklin is credited with: "A penny saved is a penny earned." Everybody likes to make money, but not as much as they love to *avoid* spending it!

So take another look at your Heart-Appeal Check List. Maybe you can make your appeals even stronger with some of this reverse English.

Again, the customer is the final test. But it's worth trying 'em both ways.

Off-Beat Approaches

In Part III we'll be taking a good long look at the various ways of using showmanship throughout your presentation. As you'll see, I'm a firm believer in this vital factor in selling. It's great to be dramatic.

But in the approach, I think the danger of trying to be *too* dramatic is even greater.

You want attention, sure. But it's got to be *favorable* attention.

A sample of the product—if it's really unusual—can sometimes be used to good advantage. Putting an entirely new kind of item on a buyer's desk is a simple form of showmanship that's perfectly O.K. In fact, if you have such a product, this may be your best approach.

A former client of ours, in the toy business, put out a totally unique kind of talking puppet. This was a natural for an offbeat approach. We found that all a salesman had to do was let the puppet do the talking!

But this was a mighty unusual situation.

In most cases, it's hard to be cleverly dramatic right off the bat. Besides, most prospects resent the salesman who is too smart.

I'll never forget a certain character who barged into my own office one day. He was clever (or fast) enough to get past the receptionist without even being announced.

He marched up to the desk, looked me straight in the eye, and barked with authority: "O.K., Mr. Wolfe, I'm from the Sheriff's office! Let's go!" Honest!

As I gaped in amazement (who wouldn't?), his face broke into a silly grin. "Ho, ho," he chuckled, "I guess I got your attention that time, didn't I?"

He sure did! I still remember him. But I don't know to this day what he was selling. I didn't wait to find out. He was out of the office quicker than he came in.

When to Make Your Opening Move

Here's where I disagree with many sales consultants. A lot of the books say you have to get right into the sale—*fast*—the minute you get within earshot of the prospect.

I say it depends. Mainly on how important *you* are in the scheme of things.

If yours is a strictly impersonal type of selling—as in a retail store or a one-shot house-to-house deal—then a wham-bam opener may be best. Here, even your own name may be completely unimportant.

But when you're selling on a fairly high level, especially if you've had some previous contact with the prospect—even indirectly—it's almost an insult to start selling right off the bat.

Of course, this doesn't mean you have to waste a half-hour of the prospect's time (as well as your own) discussing the World Series.

But in most kinds of selling you have to sell *yourself*—as well as your product—and often it's best to spend a sentence or two doing that first.

Incidentally, I happen to be pretty friendly with many of the sales consultants who dispute this.

Funny thing. When *they* sell, they do it *my* way.

Chapter 11 in a Nutshell

1. Good approaches are never canned—but always planned.
2. "How would you like to . . ."—"I've got an idea that will . . ."—"I think I can help you . . ."
3. What people **don't** want to have, they **do** want to avoid.
4. Being too off-beat puts you too off-course.
5. Get ready—get set—**then** go.

Chapter 12

KEEPING YOUR HEART-APPEALS ALIVE

Open a Sales Supermarket

Let's refer back to that Heart-Appeal Check List you've made up. With a little probing, you should have found lots of Heart-Appeals for your own product, probably at least one in each of the five categories.

Obviously, on every call, you'll want to put your emphasis on the Heart-Appeals that happen to be strongest for whatever it is you sell. The product—*your* product—is the main thing to consider.

But, as I pointed out in Part I, the *prospect* is important, too. Even with the same product, some Heart-Appeals are more potent than others. It depends on the prospect—what *he* wants.

That's why it's a good idea to open a sales supermarket— to be ready to use *whichever* Heart-Appeal has the best chance of scoring with each individual prospect.

And that, of course, is why I suggested a long time ago that you find out all you can about the prospect before you call on him.

Muzak wired music service, for instance, sells the same background music program to thousands of varied business firms throughout the country. The selections are scientifically planned so that every subscriber—in every city—gets the same carefully engineered program. The same songs, the same arrangements, the same timing. The product doesn't change.

And being businessmen, all of Muzak's customers buy for the same basic reason—*profit*. The Treasure appeal works with all of them.

But since these customers operate in many different fields, Muzak salesmen are trained to use different appeals for various prospects. I know. I've trained some of 'em!

To the restaurateur, for instance, the Muzak Selling Ace says: "Muzak adds to the atmosphere. It attracts new patrons, and brings the old ones back again."

To the store owner, he says: "Muzak makes shopping more pleasant, gets your customers to linger longer and buy more merchandise."

To the plant manager, he says: "Muzak cuts worker tension, increases production, and improves employee morale."

These are all Heart-Appeals. They all fit in the Treasure column. But they're changed to fit the prospect.

In every Muzak salesman's briefcase, there's a whole supermarket of Heart-Appeals.

You'd be wise to put the same in yours.

When to Change the Signals

Even after planning what seems to be the best approach—based on both the product *and* the prospect—sometimes individual situations require you to switch one Heart-Appeal for another.

When a football quarterback calls for a pass, it's because he believes that's his best play. Following a precise set of maneuvers, thoroughly practiced by the team, it should be good for a long gain.

But after fading back to throw, if he sees his receivers completely covered by the defense, the smart quarterback often changes his tactics, runs with the ball, and frequently dashes downfield to score.

The smart salesman is adaptable, too.

When I first started selling local radio time in Honolulu

(and I hate to think how long ago *that* was) one of my prospects was the owner of a large department store. His father had started the business, and the son—who was now the boss—was a little unsure of himself. Or so it seemed. Anyway, he just wouldn't buy. All the usual Treasure appeals—increased traffic, higher sales, and faster turnover—failed to budge him.

I finally realized that there was something this man wanted even more than financial gain—thanks to his old man, he was pretty well loaded when he started. What he *really* craved was personal success—*achievement*.

So I showed him a documentary series about successful men (narrated, incidentally, by the same fellow who in more recent years has been doing the "Millionaire" show on TV). *"This* program," I said, "will add new *prestige* to you and your store." He picked up his pen and signed a $7000 contract.

Here's the point.

All of the Heart-Appeals are important. You've got to be ready to switch signals and use whichever one applies most powerfully to your product *and* your customer.

Every Call Is Special

You've probably heard about the French girl who lived in America nine years and never learned to say "No."

Well, here's a sentence I hope *you* never learn: "I just happened to be in the neighborhood."

Because every call is important—to you *and* the prospect. If it isn't, you shouldn't be there.

So let your prospect *know* it's important—every time.

If you've planned your calls right, maybe your last stop *was* just next door. Or maybe you're making a cold call just because you noticed the office on your way out of the building. That's fine.

But don't say so!

Use your Heart-Appeals on *every* call. Because every one is special.

This presents a distinct problem to salesmen who call on the same accounts at frequent intervals. The salesman/customer relationship is apt to develop into a real buddy-buddy friendship. That's just great.

But if this is the kind of selling you do, don't fall into the trap of dropping in with a "Hi, Joe, what's new?" approach every week.

Make sure you have a *new* idea, a new slant, some new Heart-Appeal, on each and every call. Even if it isn't always easy.

For many years we've had the pleasure of working with Mutual Merchandising Cooperative, Inc., and their salesmen face this problem constantly. Except that with them it's multiplied three ways.

Mutual is an association of some 100-odd tobacco and sundries wholesalers, employing a total of well over 1000 men. These fellows call on the same stores just about every week, with a huge variety of items to sell, in a field where many outfits are selling exactly the same products and competition is fierce.

In a situation like that, how can you make "every call special"?

Well, we set up a three-point plan for these men. Here it is.

1. ONLY ONE CALL—MAKE IT COUNT! Each man was trained to forget last week and not think about next week. As soon as the salesmen began to pretend that each call was the *only* call they'd ever make on that customer—that this was "the last chance," so to speak—sales went up.

2. ONLY ONE ITEM—SPOTLIGHT IT! Similarly, the men began to sell each item individually, as if it were the only item in the line. New Heart-Appeals were presented for each piece of merchandise. Again, buyers responded with bigger orders.

3. ONLY ONE SALESMAN—YOU'RE THE STAR! This is essentially the same point we covered back in Chapter 2 of this book. By stressing personal service—the only real "exclusive" they had—Mutual's Selling Aces were able to lick competition.

These three simple points cover a lot of ground, more than I intended to include right here.

But the essential thought is the same.

Heart-Appeals are meant to be *used*—always. They never go out of style.

Chapter 12 in a Nutshell

1. Whatever you sell—sell 'em what they want to buy.
2. If you can't sell the prospect, and you can't switch the product, switch the Heart-Appeal.
3. If you walk in without a Heart-Appeal—walk out.

Chapter 13

HOW TO DEVELOP
A "YES" ATTITUDE

Decide What You Want to Sell

Every salesman knows that if you get the prospect to say (or even think) "Yes"—to anything—the battle is half won. That basic agreement is all-important.

How do you achieve it?

Well, the first step involves knowing, yourself, what you're really after, and keeping your eye on that one main objective.

What *are* you trying to sell, anyway? Are you looking for one big deal, are you aiming for a sample order, or do you simply need an O.K. to proceed with the next phase of your sales campaign?

I was once assigned the job of appointing dealers in Latin America for Mooney airplanes. Naturally, the company wanted the best possible distribution in each area. But an essential part of any deal was an order for at least one demonstrator. By letting all candidates know—right at the outset—that this was required, I was able to minimize waste time and achieve the desired results as quickly as possible. I knew I needed one big deal in each place. Knowing it—and letting others know it—I got it.

Fifi Hosiery, another of our clients, is a brand of women's stockings sold through drug and variety stores. Display racks are designed to hold three dozen, five dozen, or more. But here—as with many lines of merchandise—the size of the initial order is not of major importance. The main thing is to get the line into the store. So Fifi salesmen are provided with special incentives just to get the line placed, letting re-orders pretty much take care of themselves.

Some firms, on the other hand, use a several-stage campaign, and the first stage doesn't require an order at all. Merrill, Lynch, Pierce, Fenner & Smith, for instance, the big stock brokerage firm. These fellows don't try to "sell" anything the first time around. All they're after is an "analysis of your portfolio," on which they then base recommended transactions on the market.

So if your job falls into the first category, and you have to close the big one on the first call, keep that in mind—your mind *and* the prospect's. You'll save a lot of time if you separate the men from the boys early in the game.

If all you need is a sample order, you have a strong thing going for you. "Just try it and you'll see the results" is a strong statement. Use it.

Finally, if all you're trying to sell is a survey of some kind, you're in the best spot of all. Folks will buy almost anything "without obligation." Make it plain that this is your true position, and you're in.

Whatever you're there to sell, sell it. No more. No less.

Accentuate the Positive

Let's face it. There *are* reasons for *not* buying whatever you have to sell. You know them—or, at least, you should. If you don't, you'll find out soon enough from your prospects.

On the other side of the scale, weighing heavier, are the reasons *for* buying. And you certainly know those.

Again, this point applies throughout the sale. But it's especially important in your approach.

It's simply this:

To develop a "yes" attitude on the part of your prospect, emphasize the *plus* features you have to offer. Save your minus-factor rebuttals for later.

Another firm we've had the pleasure of serving is the City Tank Corporation, manufacturers of garbage trucks and other heavy equipment. Their Roto-Pac unit is used by city sanitation departments from New York to Mexico. Like all products, it is *not* superior in *every* way—it is simply better than the others in *most* ways.

So Roto-Pac dealers always stress the *plus* features—versatility, speed, and economy. There's always time later to answer the objections—*if* the prospect raises them.

And this brings up another extremely important point.

In Part IV we'll be talking more about objections and how to answer them. As you'll see, you needn't fear these obstacles if you know how to handle them.

But don't—don't ever—bring up the negative unless the other fellow does.

Frank Titelman, President of Puritan Sportswear, was telling me once about a salesman who came in to sell his firm some cotton fabrics for sport shirts. Without having the price questioned, this guy said: "Of course, Soandso sells their stuff cheaper." Then—and only then—he went on to explain why *his* stuff was supposed to be better.

But Frank wasn't listening. He placed his order with Soandso!

Let the prospect bring up the negatives—if he can. *You* concentrate on the positives.

Make 'Em Come to You

Have you ever tried to get rid of the family auto by driving it into a used car lot? It's a harrowing experience. The boss always seems to be in shirt sleeves, slumped in a squeaky chair, with his feet up on a battered desk. And—inevitably—there's a cigar that apparently prevents him from opening his mouth to give you the time of day. Your car is halved in value before the guy even reluctantly bothers to look at it.

And even when you go in to *buy* a car, these fellows are no pushover.

Why? Because—in both instances—you're going to *them*. It's tough to play anybody in his own ball park.

And this same principle applies in your everyday selling.

If you can get the prospect to come to *you*, you're way ahead of the game. He's got a "yes" attitude immediately—or he wouldn't be there.

Of course, you can't always get the prospect transported physically to your own office or showroom. In your business, maybe that never happens. But you can get him to come to you *figuratively*—and that's often even better.

This is a favorite technique of the International Correspondence Schools, and here's how they work it.

Let's assume that the I.C.S. salesman is visiting the home of a young fellow who inquired about the diesel engineering course. The pitch begins: "I understand you want to be a diesel engineer."

"Oh, yes, sir!" the prospect says eagerly. "I sure do!"

"That's a fine ambition," the I.C.S. Ace goes on professionally, "but what makes you think you've got what it takes to assimilate all the knowledge we're prepared to provide?"

"Gee, my foreman at the shop says I'm pretty good mechanically—and I'm willing to work at it."

"Well, that part of it's all right," counters the man from I.C.S., "but how do we know you're going to study hard enough?"

At this, the prospect's wife pipes up: "Oh, I'll get him to study!"

And so it goes—until the future engineer has "yessed" himself right into an enrollment!

Now, some of my colleagues might call this "negative selling." Maybe it is.

But it's also one of the surest ways I know to get the prospect thinking *positively* about your proposition.

Opening with the Close

I'll warn you right now this is a bold maneuver. You may not want to use it. Very honestly, I've never tried it myself.

But I know it works—for some of the real Selling Aces.

If yours is a "specialty" sale—if it's pretty much of a one-shot proposition, and the order you get *now* is the only thing that matters—give it a try.

Opening with the close simply means this: you tell the prospect plainly—almost before you begin—that you want an immediate decision.

The Encyclopedia Americana salesman says: "I'm going to tell you about our new educational plan for the family. When I get through, I want you to say Yes or No."

A leading sales training service is sold on this same basis. "I'd like twenty minutes of your time, without interruptions," the representative says. "At the end of that time I'm going to ask you for your decision."

This, of course, is exactly contrary to most selling procedures—which is why, in this book, closing techniques are discussed in Part IV.

Obviously, it smacks of high pressure.

But, like nothing else, this technique removes the "maybe" attitude so loved by so many prospects. It lays things right on the line.

Actually, it's a little like the guy at the party who propositioned every girl he met to spend a weekend with him.

"Golly," someone asked, "don't you get a lot of slaps in the face?"

"Sure," he said, "but I also get a lot of nice weekends!"

If your selling won't be hurt by a few slaps in the face, you might find this technique one of the most valuable tips in the book.

Chapter 13 in a Nutshell

1. If you can't get 'em to bite—get 'em to nibble.
2. Be positive—positively.
3. When they come to you, they come to do business.
4. Sometimes any decision is better than none.

Chapter 14

SECRETS OF SUCCESSFUL
CALL-BACKS

A New Selling Opportunity

If you were perfect—and if the techniques in this book worked *all* of the time—we wouldn't need this chapter. You'd sell everybody the first time around, and call-backs just wouldn't have to happen. What a glorious dream!

But, alas, the world isn't made up that way. Even under the fire of all the closing techniques in your arsenal (including the ones you'll get out of Part IV of this book) some people just won't jump on the first call. No matter how silly it sometimes seems, they insist on "thinking it over." Amen. That's the way the belly buttons.

But bear this important fact in mind: it's better than a flat "No."

Because, after all, you'd never get the chance at a call-back unless the guy were genuinely interested in your offering. Otherwise, you wouldn't get that second crack at him.

So the call-back is actually a new selling opportunity. Look at it that way, and you'll make more of your call-backs pay off.

Walter Benedick, President of Investors Planning Corporation, has in a few short years built one of the largest mutual funds organizations in the world. Here's what Walter said to me recently on this subject:

"I tell my men to treat second and third calls almost like the first. The prospect is bound to have forgotten much of the story. We try a new approach, a new presentation, a new close. We cover the same facts all over again if we have to—and we usually do. But we keep selling."

That last sentence offers the real clue: "But we keep selling." When making call-backs, don't take anything for granted. You may expect a "no" answer, or you may think it's in the bag. In either case, don't just go through the motions.

A call-back is a new selling opportunity. Treat it as such.

Never Ask for the Decision

This leads to Rule #1 in making call-backs pay off:

Don't—ever—merely ask for the decision.

I suppose that the huge majority of call-backs, in all fields, are made on this basis. But it's all wrong.

Here's why.

The inept salesman starts his call-back with: "Well, what have you decided about that insurance policy?"—or automobile, or typewriter, or swimming pool, or whatever.

Of course, the prospect *may* have decided "yes"—in which case everything is hunky-dory and what we're saying here isn't important.

But that doesn't happen very often. (If the prospect *had* made up his mind—definitely—to buy, he probably would have called *you*.)

It's far more likely that either one of two situations exists: (1) the prospect has pretty well decided *against* your proposal, or (2) he hasn't made a decision at all.

In either case, you'd better do some more selling if you want the deal.

And here's the important point: it's more profitable to do that selling—or, at least, as much as you can—*before* you give the other fellow a chance to throw anything negative at you.

So don't give him that chance! Don't ask him anything at all. *Tell* him something!

"Here's Something Else"

What do you tell him? *Something else.*
And the best way to do it is in just those words.
See how much better this is.
The smart salesman starts his call-back: "Say, about that insurance policy—or automobile, or typewriter, or swimming pool, or whatever—*here's something else* I didn't mention."
Then, of course, he goes on to mention the "something else" —whatever it is.
Suppose *you* try this technique next time. Here's how it will work out.
As we've analyzed, you'll be up against one of three possible situations.

1. If the prospect has already reached a favorable decision prior to your call-back, nothing will be changed. You're in.
2. If the prospect has pretty well decided *not* to buy, your "something else" *may* change his mind. At least, you have nothing to lose.
3. If no decision has been reached at all, the "something else" may well tip the balance in your favor. Anyway, you're back on the selling track.

So, at worst, you have a 1/3 better chance to score.
Worthwhile odds, wouldn't you say?

Start Where You Left Off

As I pointed out in the beginning of this Chapter, the call-back is a new selling opportunity. It calls for a new approach, and, as we've just discussed, something new must be added.
But you have one big advantage. The sale isn't *entirely* new. You've already made some progress toward a successful close, or—as we also discussed—you wouldn't get the call-back opportunity.
Obviously, if you're smart, you'll capitalize on the progress you've made.

So Rule #2 in making call-backs is: start where you left off.

What did your first interview with the prospect reveal? What did the prospect like best about your proposition? Which Heart-Appeals were most potent? What were the major objections?

All of this information, properly analyzed, will give you clues for wrapping up the sale in the next round.

I've already mentioned how the Muzak wired music people vary their Heart-Appeals to fit the prospect. But their handling of call-backs is, if anything, even better.

In Muzak's files are hundreds of letters from satisfied subscribers. As you would expect, they're arranged according to the type of firm involved: hotel, store, restaurant, bank, office, factory, etc. So, for every prospect, the salesman can always show evidence of results in other similar locations.

But, in addition, these letters are cross-referenced according to the *specific results* to which they testify. What a system!

If the prospect says: "To hell with morale, I just want my employees to turn out more widgets," the Muzak man on his next visit produces a letter that says: "Our factory production has increased 22%!"

If the prospect says: "I don't want my office girls distracted by music," the Muzak Selling Ace shows up with a letter that says: "We thought it would be distracting, but it isn't!"

We'll be talking more about this sort of selling evidence in Part III, but this particular example seemed so appropriate to the present discussion, I thought I'd include it here.

The tremendous success of Muzak's system proves the point. In making call-backs, it's smart to start where you left off.

The Sideshow-Spieler Technique

This is the best call-back technique of all. Bar none. It's so simple, so sure-fire. The only trouble is it's *too* good—the prospect may smell a rat.

And, of course, you can't always use it.

I'm referring to the method used by carnival men. You've heard 'em. Traditionally, the spiel goes like this:

"You're still not satisfied? You say you want more? Well, I'll tell you what I'm gonna do . . ."

That's all there is to it!

You tell 'em what you're going to do—and then you do whatever you have to do to get the order! (I told you it was simple.)

Let's get specific.

Let's say you failed to clinch an order because the prospect wanted it in red instead of black. You then find out you can get it in red. You call back and say: "Mr. Prospect, you said you'd buy this item if I could get it for you in red. Well, I got it!"

Or suppose you weren't able to promise delivery when the prospect demanded. You discover you can beat the required deadline. You call back and say: "Mr. Prospect, you said you wanted delivery by Septober 45th. I'll have it there by the 44th!"

Or even in the case of price. I don't believe in price-cutting, but sometimes quotations *can* be re-figured. "Mr. Prospect," you call back, "we've decided to accept your order at the exact price you offered!"

These are tough statements to argue with!

But watch out!

When you change the deal—which this technique requires— there has to be a legitimate *reason* for the change. Otherwise, it will sound phony.

As I said, this is a terrific technique, but it must be used with finesse.

Your prospect has heard of carnival men, too!

Chapter 14 in a Nutshell

1. A call-back is an approach—all over again.
2. Never ask for the decision. It might be "No."
3. If you want a new trial, present new evidence.
4. What happened last is your guide to what to do next.
5. It's great to be a sideshow spieler. But don't act like one.

PART III

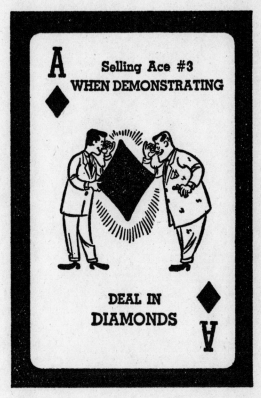

Selling Ace #3
WHEN DEMONSTRATING

DEAL IN
DIAMONDS

Chapter 15

THE MAGIC FRAME OF QUALITY

Everybody Wants the Best

In the last Part, we took a pretty good look at this fellow called Mr. Prospect. Obviously, that's necessary—after all, he's the guy we're trying to sell. You can't Hit 'Em in the Heart unless you know where to aim.

But your prospect has one other vital characteristic we didn't cover—because it properly fits in this Part. It's simply this: *everybody wants the best.* Throughout every sales presentation you ever make, it's probably *the* most important thing to remember.

This, again, is something of a paradox.

As you saw in the Heart-Appeal Check List, Treasure is a strong buying motive. People love to save money. In fact, surveys show that "free" is the strongest word used in advertising.

But nobody wants anything *cheap.* They want the *best* they can get.

Your whole presentation, therefore, must have two main objectives: first, you have to prove that your product *will* do everything you said it would during your Approach; and second, that it will do it *better* than anything else.

This Part is devoted to showing you how to do those two things.

In New York City there are dozens of cafeteria chains. Operating on a self-service basis, they all feature low prices. But the most famous of all, Horn & Hardart, is successful for another reason. Here's their slogan: "The public appreciates *quality!*"

Quality and Price—Indivisible

This is a special word to those of you who do *not* sell the best. Let's face it, not everybody can. Maybe yours is "low end" merchandise, and price is one of your strongest selling points. Don't flip too many pages! All of this quality stuff applies to *you*, too!

Because, for you, quality *and* price must go together. You can't separate 'em. Or, at least, if you do you're dead.

That's why Chevrolet has been advertising: "The car you'd want at *any* price!" Low cost is implicit in that statement—but it speaks *quality*, too.

In the appliance business, discount stores are presently enjoying a fabulous growth, primarily because of their low prices. But do you think these outfits could succeed by selling *only* price? Not on your life! They feature top brands *combined with* low prices.

Four Roses has recently come out with its new brand of Antique Bourbon. It carries a popular price tag—a natural edge over competition. But here's how the Antique Selling Aces tell it: "Antique is priced lower than other *quality* bourbons. Every bottle carries the Rour Roses reputation behind it!"

So never sell on price *alone*. That just leaves you wide open for a *real* chiseler to come along and put you out of business.

Look It—Talk It—Show It

In our Workshops around the country, we like to illustrate this business of putting a Frame of Quality around the product. What we use is a simple gold frame. This may sound silly, but putting that frame around *anything*—matches, paper clips, rubber bands, or whatever—makes that item look better.

In your own selling, there are many specific ways to create

the illusion of quality, and we'll be discussing them later in detail.

But here, in brief, are the three main points to remember:

1. *Look It.* A tramp would have a tough time selling Cadillacs. Remember, the prospect sees *you* before he sees your product. His whole attitude toward your proposition is colored by his first impression of *you.* That's why I.B.M. tells their men to wear white shirts, and why Kinney Shoe Stores have said nix to loud sport jackets. For most salesmen, this is simply a matter of common sense. You're not in uniform. But whatever you wear, let your appearance reflect the quality you want to build into your product.

2. *Talk It.* One of the glories of our nation is that we have so many varying speech patterns, both native and foreign. So I'm not suggesting that you have to emulate the mellow tones of a radio announcer. What I *do* say is that your language is another tip-off to your prospect—working for you or against you. Again, it's mainly common sense. If your language instills the prospect with confidence in *you,* that confidence will be transferred over to your product.

3. *Show It.* A salesman came into our office recently with a line of special binders for sales manuals. We use materials of this kind in making up various sorts of visual presentations for our clients, so I was interested in seeing what the man had. But get this! His *own* line was bound up in a dirty piece of brown wrapping paper! Apparently, *he* didn't think his product was very precious—so why should I? Contrast this with the impression created by a crackerjack typewriter salesman I know. Before setting the machine down on his prospect's desk, this Selling Ace always removes a snow-white handkerchief from his breast pocket, breathes on it lightly, then gently wipes off the already-spotless typewriter! How's *that* for showing quality!

The whole point is this:

We've established the importance of building quality in the mind of the prospect.

O.K. Everything you say, everything you do—*everything*

about you—either helps to strengthen, or to destroy, the impression you're trying to create.

So put a Frame of Quality around your product—*all* around—and let that quality shine through.

Chapter 15 in a Nutshell

1. Sell the best. It's none too good—but anything less is too bad.
2. Selling price is O.K.—if you sell quality along with it.
3. Look quality, talk quality, show quality. The frame blocks out competition.

Chapter 16

HOW TO DEVELOP
TALKING POWER

Words Work Wonders

This chapter is devoted to one thing—*words*.

In the last chapter, we took an over-all look at *all* the factors that contribute to building an image of quality. Why? Because the image must be a *whole* image—and the whole is the sum of *all* its parts.

But, getting down to the bare bones, a salesman is—primarily—a *talking* animal. The most important factor, throughout your presentation, is what you *say*. The ultimate weapon in your arsenal—and the most devastating—is your tongue.

So a whole chapter on the subject is well deserved.

Again, not knowing the specific product or service you sell, I can't tell you exactly which words to use. But I can give you an idea as to the *kinds* of words you'll find most effective, and how to *use* them profitably.

Here are three general rules to follow:

1. *Use frisky words—avoid lazy words.* That automobile you're selling: it doesn't "go" up hills—it *zooms!* That new airliner: it doesn't "carry" you to your destination, or even "speed" you—it *whisks* you! Or take any good product sold for resale: it doesn't "move" off the shelves—it *leaps!*

2. *Use "garden-variety" words—avoid "Phi Beta Kappa key" words.* A premium doesn't come to you "without charge"—it's

free! A new business machine doesn't do the work "expeditiously"—it does it *fast!* And even the ideas in this book: don't "utilize" them—*use* them!

3. *Use "for-sure" words—avoid "maybe" words.* Don't say: "If you had our heater, you would save money on your fuel bills." Say: "With our heater you *will* save money on your fuel bills!" Junk the subjunctive! It's great for English teachers—but lousy for salesmen.

Remember, some words sell—some don't. Use the ones that do.

Talk in Three Dimensions

We've been talking about words. You use words—lots of them—every time you make a sales presentation.

But you wouldn't if you didn't have to!

What I mean is this:

If you could *show* your prospect all the benefits of your product—the benefits he'll enjoy *after* buying it—there'd be darn little left to say.

You can, of course, demonstrate the product—and we'll be talking more about that in the next chapter. But you can't physically project the prospect into tomorrow.

So you do it with words.

This means, therefore, that you have to create a three-dimensional picture of what's going to happen *after* the purchase is made. And the more *complete* you make the picture, the better.

That's why the swimming pool salesman says: "Just imagine a glamorous free-form pool right there by the patio! Your house will be the showplace of the neighborhood! And if you ever decide to sell the house, its market value will be increased far beyond the low cost of our pool!"

Of course, you may say that it's a little easier to get ecstatic about a swimming pool than it is with the particular product you're selling. That may be.

But whatever you sell, use words that make *pictures.*

Put the Prospect in the Picture

In that imaginary picture of the swimming pool, there's one thing we've left out—the most important thing of all.

The prospect!

Without *him* the picture isn't complete—nowhere near it.

So going back to the swimming pool salesman, here's how he goes on: "And when *you* come home after a hard day in the sweltering city, think what a joy it will be to just dash through the house, jump into the pool, and relax in those cool waters! All summer long, without spending a dime or traveling a mile, *you* will enjoy resort-living, right here in your own back yard!"

By this time, the salesman has his prospect mentally stripped to his BVD's, ready to take a plunge!

You can do the same thing with any product, tangible or intangible.

My friend Charlie Barton, President of the C. B. Knight Insurance Agency in New York, said this recently: "I tell my men to paint a word picture of a financially secure family, of the home fully paid for, of kids graduating from college. We ask the prospect how *he* would like to spend his retirement years, if he lives, and then let him picture himself enjoying those pleasures without a worry in the world!"

That may be one reason why C. B. Knight is the largest insurance agency in the country!

So why don't *you* try it? Just paint a picture—then put the *prospect* in it.

Keep the Heart Beating

Just one final word on words.

Part II was all about Heart-Appeals. It stressed the importance of using those Heart-Appeals every time you begin a sales presentation—"In Every Approach, Hit 'Em in the Heart!"

But the use of those Heart-Appeals is not limited to the approach. Don't throw 'em away, just because you're into the guts of your presentation.

Keep coming back to them!

For several years we've had the pleasure of running sales meetings and Selling Aces Workshop sessions for the American Express Company. Thanks largely to the splendid leadership of Senior Vice President George Waters, the American Express Credit Card is the undisputed top credit credential in the world. In selling their credit card plan to fine restaurants and hotels, the American Express Aces naturally use Treasure as their strongest appeal—the extra *profits* to be made.

And they don't let anyone forget it! They keep the Heart beating!

In discussing their various promotional aids, they'll say: "The name of your establishment will be right in front of people when they're looking for a truly fine place to entertain. This way, we bring you plus business!"

In explaining how the payment plan operates, they'll point out: "We guarantee prompt payment in full, twice every month. You never have to wait for your money!"

And when it comes to describing their cardholders, they'll always emphasize: "These are all successful people. They're the folks who'll spend the most in your place of business!"

Get the idea?

Throughout your presentation—whatever particular feature of the product you may be discussing—*relate* that feature to a strong Heart-Appeal.

That way, you keep the Heart beating—and you put more power in your presentation.

Chapter 16 in a Nutshell

1. Words work wonders—if they're the right words.
2. If the prospect can't see it, you can't sell it.
3. You're not the star of the picture—the prospect is.
4. If the prospect's Heart stops beating, you're the one who's dead.

Chapter 17

THERE'S NO BUSINESS
LIKE "SHOW" BUSINESS

Transmit on All Five Channels

In Chapter 15, right at the start of this Part, we touched on the importance of *showing* your prospect—as well as telling him—what you have to offer. The more "show" you put into your presentation, the more impact it will have—for many reasons. When *Demonstrating*, Deal in Diamonds.

After all, selling is mainly a matter of *communication* between you and the fellow you're trying to sell. The more lines of communication you set up, the better your chances of coming in loud and clear, and the more you'll sell.

There's another factor to this business of show business, too. It sets you apart from your competitors.

As you're perfectly well aware, you're not the only salesman on the street. That prospect of yours has heard sales talks before—lots of 'em. But with the right kind of *showmanship*, you can make your presentation *different* from all the rest. Your product will be remembered—and *you'll* be remembered.

So let's take a look at some of the specific ways to use showmanship in your selling.

As you know, every normal human being has five senses. These are the five "channels" on which you can—and should—broadcast:

HEARING. Obviously, everything you say—and the way you say it—comes over this channel. But, in terms of showmanship, you can transmit far more than words.

The smart automobile salesman, for instance, opens and closes the car door several times. He lets you *hear* the solid construction.

The clever TV Selling Ace demonstrates the strength of the picture tube by giving it a hard slap with the palm of his hand. You *see* him do it, of course, but it's the loud "thwack" in your *ear* that makes this such a powerful demonstration.

My friend H. B. "Doc" Sharer, a top executive at U. S. Rubber Company, is one of the cleverest sales trainers I know. At his suggestion, when demonstrating U. S. Royal tires, the salesman always slams the car around a sharp corner, whispering: "Sh! You can almost *hear* the quiet!" And you can!

SIGHT. Which is more powerful: an eye image, or an ear image? Dozens of surveys show that what you *see* hits you harder than what you hear. The percentages aren't important. To you, as a salesman, what *is* important is this: When your prospect can *see* the benefits of your proposition, *and* hear about it *at the same time*, you've got *two* things going for you, with *at least double* the impact.

Example: a good half-hour radio show can be broadcast nationally for about *one-tenth* the cost of the same show on TV. An evening half-hour on the NBC radio network, for instance, costs $7620. For NBC TV, the figure is $75,000. And production costs vary to the same extent. Yet companies will pay this tremendous premium—just to get their sales message *seen* by the public, as well as heard.

This is why the vacuum cleaner Selling Ace always offers to clean your rugs, to *show* what his machine will do. And why the fire extinguisher salesman always starts a small fire in a waste-basket—when you *see* the extinguisher in action, it means more than anything the salesman could ever say.

Shortly after the end of World War II, I happened to drive past a certain used car lot in Oklahoma City. I was lucky enough to own a post-war car, and needed a new one like a hole in the head. But there, sitting proudly in the center of

the lot, was a shiny new Ford Sportsman, the swanky con-
vertible with the wood body. It also had electric windows,
quite an innovation in those days. Remember?

At any rate, I drove in and asked the salesman how much
he wanted in trade. When he told me, I *knew* I didn't need it,
and I said so.

I'll never forget that man's technique. He didn't say anything! All the so-and-so did was play with those blasted windows—up and down, up and down, up and down. My ears
heard nothing, but my eyes were working like a yo-yo. I
remember thinking to myself: "Anybody who spends that kind
of money for that car is a damned fool!"

P.S. It turned out to be a pretty good car. I kept it for
years.

FEEL. Not every salesman can transmit on this channel, because some products just don't lend themselves to its use. But
if yours is a product whose superiority *can* be *felt*—as well as
heard and seen—take advantage of it.

In luggage, for instance, weight is an important considera-
tion. The smart luggage salesman lets the customer *feel* how
little the item weighs, how easy it is to carry.

Another of our clients is Blume Knitwear, Inc., manufacturers of Helen Harper sweaters. Barnett Lerner, president of
the firm, says that good looks and long wear are not the only
qualities they sell. The sweaters that *feel* better, *sell* better.

What golfer would ever buy a set of clubs without testing
to see how they *feel* in the swing?

And feel applies importantly to packaging, too. Manufacturers of many kinds of household products spend millions of
dollars every year to develop tubes and jars that *feel* better
in the hand. It's an important part of the sales story.

TASTE AND SMELL. These last two senses are still more limited
in their use as channels for sales messages. Again, if you can't
use them, you can't—if you can, they're probably the most
important of all.

Food products, beverages, and tobacco all sell—or fail to sell
—primarily on the basis of taste. Perfumes, and other similar
products, rely on smell.

But these senses *are* important to some other products as well.

Does the aroma of a bath soap have anything to do with its cleaning power? I don't know. Does a sweet-tasting tooth paste prevent more cavities? You tell me.

But I *do* know that these factors affect the *sale* of these products, and that's what we're concerned with.

The point is simply this:

You're a salesman, with a message to get across to your prospect. You want to do it as accurately and as forcefully as possible. You wouldn't stuff his ears with cotton, would you? Well, blocking out any of the other senses—by ignoring them—is almost as bad.

So transmit on as many channels as you can—all five, if possible.

Let the Other Fellow Get into the Act

In Chapter 16, talking about talk, I mentioned the importance of putting the prospect in the picture. That goes double here. Wherever possible, put the prospect in the *show*, too.

There are two reasons for this.

First, when *he* does it, *he* understands it. Even more importantly, he *believes* it. People are inherently a little suspicious of all salesmen (even you!)—but when you let the prospect prove something *to himself,* he's *got* to go along with you.

This is why the automobile salesman lets *you* drive the car. When your *own* toe on the gas pedal gives you that feel of power, it means far more than any fancy driving exhibition put on by the salesman.

Similarly, the typewriter Selling Ace lets the buyer (or, even more importantly, his secretary) type out a letter. That's the only real test.

This is one of the points we stressed in the training films we made for the J. J. Newberry Company. For instance, when the salesgirl says, "See how this new material springs back to shape!" she lets the *customer* try bunching it up in her own hands. Then there's no doubt.

Have you ever seen one of those sharpies demonstrating a trick deck of cards at a carnival? In *their* hands, everything looks so simple, yet so amazing. Take it home, and you're ready to swear it's a different piece of goods. Why? Because you didn't have a chance to try it, *yourself*, first.

The second reason for letting the other fellow get into the act is even more basic: simply because he *wants* to.

It's for this same reason that fathers buy electric trains for their two-year-old sons. (Not having a son, I bought one for our dog!) We're all boys at heart.

So if your presentation involves a demonstration of some clever gadget, and the other guy wants to play—let him!

As Jimmy Durante says: "*Everybody* wants to get into the act!" You can't afford to be a prima donna.

Some years ago, I was connected with Mooney Aircraft, manufacturers (at that time) of a small, single-seat airplane. The only way to demonstrate the airplane's capabilities was to let the prospect fly it—alone. All the salesman could do was sit on the ground, cross his fingers, and pray fervently. Occasionally, a prospect would grin sheepishly and apologize for forgetting to put the wheels down, as he crawled out of the wreckage, but that was one of the hazards of the business.

You have to let the other fellow get into the act.

How to Demonstrate Intangibles

So far, in this chapter, we've been talking mostly about tangible products. If you happen to sell a so-called "intangible" service—such as insurance, mutual funds, advertising, etc.—you may be wondering what all this has to do with you. Right now, you may be saying: "What I sell *can't* be seen, or felt, or tasted, or smelled. How do *I* demonstrate?"

O.K. Let's talk about *you*.

First of all, let's get this straight. *Every* product or service can be demonstrated in some way—including yours.

In fact, a lively piece of showmanship may be more necessary in *your* case than it would be if you were selling a tangible product.

Since the product itself *can't* be seen, you've *got* to put *something* in front of the other fellow that *can* be.

How? Simply by using some sort of tangible symbol to represent the benefits of the intangible service.

The Student Marketing Institute, here in New York, specializes in helping manufacturers build distribution on college campuses across the country. It's a highly "intangible" service, quite unique, and, hence, somewhat hard to explain to a prospect. S.M.I. account executives carry a special "key"—similar to a Phi Beta Kappa key. Laying it on his prospect's desk, the account man says: "Right here is your key to the tremendous college market in America!" Simple? Sure! But that key symbolizes everything S.M.I. has to sell.

At Investors Planning Corporation, one of the leading mutual funds organizations, many Selling Aces use torn dollar bills to demonstrate their "product." Placing the torn-in-half bill in front of the prospect, the salesman says: "If inflation continues the way it's been going, this is what each of your savings account dollars is apt to be worth when you retire!" Placing a crisp whole new dollar next to it, the Ace continues: "But with mutual funds, your dollars keep up with the times!"

Fritz Kleene, head of the Home Insurance Company back in Hawaii, told me of a cute demonstration he's used to good effect in the field. He made up a small, simple sort of picture puzzle. One piece was labeled, "Job"—another, "Home"—another, "Savings," etc. "This is a picture of your financial future," Fritz would tell his prospect. Putting in the pieces, he'd say: "You've got a good job, you own a home, you've accumulated some savings. But you need *insurance* to tie the whole picture together!"—and in went the last, big, interlocking piece! Clever, huh?

But I think Charlie Barton, President of the C. B. Knight Agency, really has the answer. As he told me recently, "We're not selling an 'intangible' at all! What's more tangible than money? If the guys in this business could only realize that ours *is* a tangible product, they'd sell a lot more insurance."

So that's it! Just make your product *tangible* in the eyes of the prospect!

Your Magic Wand

I'm going to close this Chapter with the simplest kind of demonstration imaginable.

Besides being simple—which is a good thing in itself—this method has two great advantages: (1) you can use it with any product, tangible or intangible; and (2) it works.

All it takes is a pencil.

Let's say you're selling a piece of equipment that costs $900. Its normal life is 5 years. You take out your pencil and start figuring, as follows: "Hm! Let's see. Five years is sixty months. Sixty into $900—why, that's only $15 a month! That's all it'll cost you to enjoy the benefits of this machine!"

Of course, you knew darn well it would work out to $15 a month. But you don't say it—you *figure* it, on paper.

Or turn it around the other way.

Suppose you're selling an item requiring monthly payments of $15. Again using pencil and paper, you figure, as follows: "Hm! Let's see. There are thirty days in a month. Thirty into $15—why, that's only 50¢ a day! That's all it'll cost you to enjoy the benefits of this machine!"

You can use this same gimmick in figuring insurance benefits, time savings, profits—anything!

Somehow, it's impressive. Your pencil is truly a magic wand.

By the way, there's another reason for getting your pencil out.

It's handy for writing orders.

Chapter 17 in a Nutshell

1. All five senses make sense—and dollars.
2. Put on a show—with audience participation.
3. Intangibles aren't.
4. The deal can be sold—when you stop to figure it.

Chapter 18

TUNE IN YOUR SALES RADAR

You Can't Climb a Ladder Without Rungs

Chapter 16 was entitled, "How to Develop Talking Power." We might call this one, "How to Develop *Listening* Power."

As we've said, selling is mainly a matter of communication between you and the prospect. If you're going to sell successfully, that communication has got to go in both directions. It can't be a one-way street.

In Part II, I pointed out how most people are pretty much alike. Basically, they want the same things, the same *basic* things that your product offers. That's why it's possible—and, in most cases, advisable—to standardize on your approaches, and, hence, why your Heart-Appeal Check List can be so helpful.

But when you get on into the guts of your presentation, it's a different story. You have to get the prospect to do some of the talking.

You see, by this time, necessarily, you're discussing details. And when it comes to *details*, people *are* different. And, once again, because you have to sell the prospect—*not* the product—you have to find out what *he* is thinking.

How? Simply by asking.

"Now that I've given you a rough idea as to what our machine can do for you," says the business machine salesman, "tell me: what do *you* think of it? It's really some machine, isn't it?"

A question like this will usually get the guy talking. But not always. Sometimes all you get is a grunt. What then? Ask another question.

"Well, naturally, we build our machines to fit *all* offices. Some features are more important to certain people than others. In terms of your own office situation here at the XYZ Company, which of these features strikes *you* best?"

Of course, most people *like* to express their opinions. Usually, it isn't necessary to pry words out of the prospect. Some of 'em give you too many! Here, we're talking mainly about the guys who *don't* say much—which is worse.

Naturally, occasionally you run into a prospect who fibs. He tells you things that don't really reflect his true thinking. In this case, you just have to be a good enough detective to ferret out the truth—without calling him a liar.

Another toughy is the guy who loves to talk about everything except your proposition. He'll keep you there all week if you let him. This sort of activity fills the air with profound statements, but it doesn't do much to fill order books. The best procedure with this joker is to go along with him just a little of the way—to keep him from getting mad at you—and then to swing back into the sale. Don't get sidetracked.

The more you get the prospect to talk—*if* he talks honestly and *if* he talks on the subject—the more you'll sell.

Aim Your Questions at the Order Book

Most salesmen are familiar with the "which" method of closing the sale—closing on a choice. (If you're not, you'll find it covered thoroughly in Part IV.)

But this technique is not limited to the close. You can use it throughout your presentation. It's a beautifully insidious thing.

Without asking the prospect to commit himself (which, obviously, is required in the close)—he does! Or, at least, part way.

We used to find this technique effective in selling Muzak, back in Hawaii. As you know, Muzak is a specially-planned program of background music, piped over telephone wires, for stores, restaurants, offices, factories, etc. Ultimately, of course, the music comes out through loudspeakers which are installed at the location. In Hawaii, in addition to the standard Muzak program of popular selections, we also sold a special program of Hawaiian music, for hotels and other tourist attractions where this was preferred.

Therefore—even if we already knew the answer—we'd always ask: "Which type of music do you feel would fit best here: Hawaiian or the standard program?"

Note that a straight answer doesn't *necessarily* commit the prospect. He can logically have a preference and still not buy. But it's a sure step forward!

Then we might ask: "I wonder how many loudspeakers we'd need here. What do *you* think?"

Again, the question itself meant little. We had a formula all worked out, based on the size of the location, that gave us the answer. But the way the *prospect* answered the question told us a lot!

You don't have to throw the big question at 'em all at once. Try a few small ones on for size first.

The "How Am I Doing?" Technique

This is pretty similar to what we've been talking about. So far, all of the examples in this chapter fit into the broad category of this method.

But, strictly speaking, there's this difference: the "How Am I Doing?" technique lets you find out what you need to know— under the right conditions—*without* making the prospect do any real talking.

When do you use it? When that's all you need to determine —how you're doing!

When I first got out of Dartmouth, before I went back to Honolulu, I took a three-month job selling a special promotional radio program in San Francisco. It was sold entirely by telephone, using a canned pitch, typed out in advance, and delivered almost word for word. (Normally, I'm dead set against a completely canned pitch, but, I must confess, this one worked miracles.)

At any rate, by its very nature, this sale required the prospect to say virtually nothing. So "How Am I Doing?" questions were strategically spotted throughout.

After a long description of the special booklet around which the promotion was built, we'd say (following the script): "That's quite a book, isn't it?"

"Sure sounds like it," would come over the wire—and the pitch would go on.

Later, after building up the promotion at great length, we'd read this line: "Isn't that a worthwhile program?"

"I guess it is," the prospect would get in edgewise—and off we'd go again.

In fairness to myself, I must point out that I was a pretty naive kid at the time, and didn't know the whole thing was as phony as a three-dollar bill. Otherwise, I'm sure I would not have been so successful selling it.

But I think this does point out the value of the basic technique. When all you want to know is "How Am I Doing?"—ask the guy!

If you find out you're doing O.K., just keep selling.

When you need to know more, ask more.

And one final word to this chapter:

When the other guy is talking—*listen*.

When you listen hard, you sell easy.

Chapter 18 in a Nutshell

1. The prospect has a mind—and a mouth. Let him use both.
2. Like in school—give 'em the easy questions first.
3. Keep asking, "How Am I Doing?"—and you'll keep doing O.K.

Chapter 19

PROVING YOUR CASE

Make Every Link Unbreakable

A chain, they say, is as strong as its weakest link. If one link breaks—just *one*—so does the entire chain.

Well, every sale is essentially a chain of persuasion. So the analogy is valid: one weak link in your sales story can ruin the whole deal.

Let's review a little.

During the last few chapters, I've been doing my best to help you put more power into your presentation. With words and actions, your aim is to persuade the prospect that he'd darn well better buy this thing from you, or he'll hate himself in the morning.

But telling him—even showing him—is not enough. Before you can safely ask for the order, you have to make absolutely sure that he *believes* your story. You've got to *prove* that your product is worth more than his money.

That's what this chapter is all about.

Of course, we've touched on this before.

Way back in Part I, you'll remember, I said that the more you know about your business, the more confidence the prospect will have in everything you say.

Then, just two chapters ago, I said that when you let the other fellow get into the act, your demonstration becomes far more persuasive.

But the main thing to remember is this: some things *can't* be proved, because they aren't so. These are the weak links you have to watch out for. So don't say—or even imply—*anything* you can't back up 100%.

Don't bluff—ever. If the prospect catches you telling even one little fib, he'll doubt everything else you've said.

Make every link unbreakable.

Understatement Wins Confidence

Even where you do have honest-to-goodness facts to back up your statements, it's often smart strategy to *underplay* your hand, rather than overplay it.

People are suspicious of a product—just as they are of a person—that is *too* good.

We are presently engaged in developing sales for Vanguard Solid Lubricants, makers of Graphyglyde. The automotive industry has been plagued with a succession of oil additives— some good, some not so good—all of which claim miracles. Graphyglyde happens to do more than all the rest, but we tell the salesmen to softpedal some of its benefits. Why? Because we know the soft approach is more apt to be believed.

Or take a look at some of the ads for Volkswagen cars. No dreamy pictures, no exaggerated claims—just simple, straightforward facts about a good product. Volkswagen "Deals in Diamonds"—but softly. That's probably one reason for the car's fabulous sales success against tough Detroit competition.

(Notice, I didn't say it was the *only* reason. If I had, you wouldn't have believed me!)

In fact, we use this same technique constantly in our own business.

Just last week I was discussing a proposed selling plan with Mr. R. L. Anderson, Personnel Manager of the Kinney shoe store chain, another of our clients. At one point I remarked: "Some of your 500 stores may not get a great deal of benefit out of this program, but I'm pretty sure *most* of them will get a lot." To which he replied: "Heck, *almost all* of them need it!"

If I had claimed to perform miracles for *every* store, the reaction might have been: "Oh, yeah! There's one in East Beltbuckle that wouldn't touch this idea with a ten-foot pole!"

With understatement, you get a positive response. With overstatement, it's negative.

And never forget: everything you say is important, but it's *the prospect's reaction* to what you say that really counts.

Material Witness Selling

Here, now, is *the* way to put real proof into your presentation. No qualification needed here—this technique beats 'em all.

And, like all good methods, it's simple.

Essentially, "material witness selling" means letting *somebody else* clinch your deal for you. It's the best way to prove anything.

For example, could you imagine a prosecuting attorney getting up in court and saying something like this? "Gentlemen of the jury, *I* am convinced that this guy shot his wife, and, therefore, you ought to convict him!" He wouldn't have much of a case, would he?

But when the "other woman" gets up and says: "He told me he hated the old bag!"

And the ballistics expert testifies: "The bullet came from his gun!"

And the neighbor swears: "I saw him do it!"

Then the prosecutor has a pretty good case.

Same way in selling. No matter what you say, no matter what you do, nothing—but nothing—is as persuasive as the testimony of someone else.

This is why Muzak's call-back system, described in Chapter 14, is so effective. The Muzak Selling Ace is armed with testimonial letters from satisfied users, *proving* Muzak's benefits in situations identical to each prospect's.

Again, take a look at the ads. (I keep referring to advertising, but with good reason. Don't forget that the fellows who write copy are salesmen, too—good ones.)

In just one recent issue of *U.S. News and World Report,* Moore Business Forms used a testimonial from Celanese Chemical Company, Burroughs Corporation used one from Pittsburgh Plate Glass Company, Armco Steel used one from Stockton Marine, Bodine Motors used one from Haloid Xerox, Eastman Chemical Products used one from Carborundum Company, and Shaw-Walker Office Equipment used one from Surety Life Insurance Company! Wow! In some cases, the executive of the testifying firm even had his picture in the ad, as well as his name!

And don't think this isn't red-hot ammunition for the salesmen who are out in the field pushing the products to which all this testimony is being given! I don't happen to know very much about the particular firms in question, or their bosses, but if they aren't getting their men to *use* this testimony in the field, they're nuts. It's powerful stuff.

A final, clever wrinkle to this business of using testimonials has been added by the George S. May Company, the large consulting firm. In their literature, testimonial letters are *notarized.* What could be more impressive than that? Here's an idea that costs pennies, but it pays off big in sales results.

So if somebody else thinks your product is good—and there *must* be *somebody*—use this in your selling. The other fellow's opinion means more (to the prospect) than yours.

Examine the Witness

There's just one more point to this material witness selling —you've got to pick the right witness.

Again going back to the courtroom analogy, certain witnesses add more proof than others. It depends who they are. No matter how valid their testimony might otherwise be, few cases are won on the strength of the words of a gangster, or a drunkard, or the village idiot.

So, wherever possible, use witnesses who are: (1) known, and (2) respected. The witness must be at least equal in stature to the prospect you're trying to sell.

Therefore, if you're attempting to sell a line of merchandise to a small-town department store, it's quite impressive to cite the success of your goods at Macy's in New York, or Marshall Field in Chicago. But if you try to sell the Macy's or Marshall Field buyer on the basis of what happened in Podunk, you won't have much luck.

An even worse policy is mentioning, as witness, an outfit outwardly disliked, such as a too-close (and/or too-tough) competitor. Business neighbors *can*, of course, be the best of friends. But, all too often, if you tell your prospect that his competitor across the street likes it, you'll hear: "Oh, yeah! Well, if that so-and-so bought it, I hope it chokes him!" And about all you can do then is back meekly out the door.

So examine the witness before you put him on the stand.

I remember a young guy who once applied to us for a job. Basically, he seemed to be a pretty good man, fully qualified to do the work required, and we were seriously considering putting him on. Then I asked him for a couple of personal references.

"No trouble at all," he said, "just call Bill Smith. Here's his number."

"Fine," I said, reaching for the phone. "But one small question: who's Bill Smith?"

"Oh, you've never heard of him. He's just my neighbor. Drives a truck. But he's known *me* for years!"

(This is a true story—honest!)

The moral is obvious: the witness must be someone whose name—or, at least, reputation—*means something* to the man you're trying to convince.

If it does, you'll find your material witness the best salesman you ever saw.

Better, even, than *you!*

Chapter 19 in a Nutshell

1. Stronger links make stronger chains—and bigger sales.
2. The softer you speak—the harder you sell.
3. Let the other fellow sell for you. It's easier—and better.
4. Avoid hostile witnesses—and you avoid hostile prospects.

Chapter 20

HOW TO SELL UP

Never Underestimate the Buyer

For some salesmen, this chapter may be extraneous. If you have only one item to sell, which never changes as to quality or quantity, then this is not for you.

But that's a rare situation. For most men, orders can vary. They can be big or small. If this is true with you—as it probably is—obviously, you'd like *bigger* sales, as well as more sales.

So a chapter on this is worthwhile.

And the first rule is: never underestimate the buyer. You have to think as big as he thinks.

This, obviously, has to do with your own attitude. Once you've determined that this prospect can buy (and pay for) your product at all, make two more decisions: (1) that he can buy *plenty* of it, if he wants to; and (2) that you want *at least* your fair share of his business. It's simply a matter of setting your sights high enough.

Jack Kaduson, Vice-President of Four Roses Distillers, gave me an interesting slant on this the other day. Here's what he said:

"Our salesmen are often called 'missionary' men, and just as often I wish they weren't. The fellows who build business for us are real *salesmen*. They let their outlets know they want *more*, and they get it. And that's what we like. The 'missionaries' just walk around carrying the gospel"

So don't fall into the trap of being just a "missionary" man.

They say it's bad to overload your customer, and that's true. But it's worse to underload him. *Somebody* is getting real business out of that prospect. Why shouldn't it be you?

Sell the Breed—Not the Brand

Way back in Part I, we talked about ways to lick competition. And that's important. Certainly, nobody wants to give business to his competitor. Let him starve!

But sometimes the best way to build your own business is to increase sales for *all* products in the field. And if this results in a little more business slopping over to your competitor, who cares? All you're really interested in is what *you* get out of it.

And that can be plenty.

A good example of this is the strategy now being used by the Blume Knitwear outfit, makers of Helen Harper women's sweaters.

We recently ran a three-day sales meeting for this firm. Our theme for the meeting, as well as for the entire promotional program, was: "The Golden Era." In line with all Helen Harper advertising, the salesmen's main pitch is that sweaters *in general* are being sold in greater and greater numbers and, hence, that each store should build up its sweater department. The men sell sweaters first, Helen Harper second. But you can be darn sure the Helen Harper Aces get at least their fair share. If some of the other sweater outfits also receive a little benefit from this program, so what? Helen Harper gets more.

In selling the over-all "breed," some smart manufacturers widen their horizons even further. This is especially true with outfits in the supermarket field, where it's almost impossible to get preferred display space, or any other special push, for a single item.

This is why Quality Bakers of America, another of our clients, plans general, all-round promotions to stimulate sales for their Sunbeam Bread. During one season it may be a Back-To-School "Lunch Box" Promotion, during another it may be a "Picnic Pickings" Program, etc. In this way, Quality Bakers helps the stores sell many vastly different products. The important thing is that the stores sell (and, hence, buy) more bread. And, again, sales go up for Sunbeam.

In many cases, as indicated by these examples, a lot can be accomplished when over-all company policy is directed along these lines. Clever planning at the top is certainly a big help. (And you never know—maybe your boss is reading this, too!)

But even if your firm doesn't use this strategy on a company-wide basis, *you* can. And it will pay off.

So if you sell barbecue equipment, try to get your accounts to set up an "Outdoor Living" department.

If you sell hardware, both you *and* your customers will benefit if they open a "Do-It-Yourself" department.

If you sell games, you might suggest a "Family Fun Center" for each store.

Doing all of this on your own hook will do two things:

First, by building sales for your customers, you'll build sales for yourself. Whatever anybody says, there *is* honor among buyers—they'll remember it was *your* suggestion that increased their business.

And second, by starting something that stimulates sales as effectively as this does, you're apt to become a real hero within your own company.

And what's wrong with that?

Small Increases Make Big Sales

This whole chapter is about bigger sales, and how to make them. We're not concerned here with *the* sale—we're talking about increasing a sale that's already been made.

And that's one of the nicest things about this kind of selling. Once a guy has decided to buy *something* from you, it's not too hard, usually, to get him to buy more.

If you take it step by step.

Our first Selling Aces Workshop in Houston was for the Houston Natural Gas Company, whose residential sales department is headed by a real Selling Ace, Rolland Storey. You don't always think of a utility company as selling "multiple lines," but Rolland's men found this an ideal technique to use.

Let's assume that the builder of a new apartment project has called the Gas Company to help plan the heating installation. The salesman has arrived, and the heating system has been arranged for.

At this point, the Ace is apt to say: "Your apartments will rent more quickly if you install modern gas appliances in every kitchen!" The owner agrees.

Then the Ace might say: "You'll have happier tenants if you give them the added convenience of clean-burning gas grills out in the back!" This is a good idea, and the owner goes along.

But the Ace isn't through. "Now with all those grills back there, you certainly ought to make sure there's enough light for the folks to see what they're cooking. Let's give 'em the warm glow of a permanent gas light alongside each grill!"

And so it goes.

Notice, at no time does the Ace suggest that the buyer order five times as much as he intended. That's what ultimately happens, of course, but only because it happens *bit by bit*. Otherwise it wouldn't.

So when you're looking for a big order, *start small*. Then build. It's easier that way.

There is, of course, a final straw that will break any camel's back. But if you pile on the straws *piece by piece*, the camel can hold quite a bundle. Drop a whole stack of hay all at once, and the back will break much sooner.

Remember the old Chinese proverb: "A trip of a thousand miles begins with a single step."

Chapter 20 in a Nutshell

1. If the buyer can buy a little, he can probably buy a lot.
2. When you sell the breed, you sell the brand.
3. Nobody will give you a million dollars—but they may give you a dollar a million times.

Chapter 21

SECRETS IN SELLING MULTIPLE LINES

Put 'Em All in the Center Ring

How long since you've seen a three-ring circus? Years, maybe.

But I'll bet you still remember the utter confusion that filled the tent when all three rings were going at once. No *one* act stood out. It was just a big, busy mass (or was it a mess?) of entertainment.

Of course, that's the way it was planned. You weren't *supposed* to concentrate on any single performer.

That is, not until the real *star* appeared. Then things were different! When the main attraction went on—the lion tamer, high-wire acrobats, or girl shot from a cannon—the lights were dimmed, everything was quiet in the outside rings, and all attention was glued to that *one* act spotlighted in the center ring.

Well, if you're a man who sells a variety of items, there's only one way to do it—put 'em *all* in the center ring. You've got to make *every* item the star attraction.

In planning training programs for our client, Mutual Merchandising Cooperative, Inc., I've had the opportunity of working with many of the men in the field. The Mutual organization consists of over 100 tobacco and sundries jobbers throughout the country. Their salesmen, about 1000 in all, sell everything from cigarettes to sun glasses. Their catalogs bulge with ball pens, flashlights, combs, wallets, pocket knives, watch bands, etc., etc.

Unfortunately, *some* of these men still operate like a three-ring circus. They bombard the buyer with too many items all at once. What happens? The customer can't concentrate on *anything*. And, of course, if he can't concentrate, he can't buy.

But the *good* men—Mutual's Selling Aces—put *every* item in the spotlight. Items are shown and talked about *one at a time*. And while each one is being discussed, no reference is made to any other. Each is sold *as if it were the only item in the line*.

Sure, in every salesman's line, some items are stronger than others. But your job is to sell 'em all—or, at least, as many as you can—on each call. And the only way to do it is to give *each one* the full treatment.

How? By putting 'em all in the center ring.

Start Writing—and Keep At It

This is really a corollary to the gas firm's technique, described in the last chapter. Actually, whether you're trying to sell more of one line, or more of many lines, it works about the same.

The idea is simply to start writing an order the minute your customer gives you the first teensy-weensy crumb, and then to keep adding as much as you can as you go along. You don't wait until you're finished. You write up each part of the order *as you get it*.

One of the best exponents of this technique that I've ever seen is Tommy Hopkins. Tommy is a manufacturers' representative in Honolulu, carrying a large variety of lines of consumer goods.

When a buyer walks into Tommy's showroom (or hotel suite when he is on the road), Tommy asks: "Which line would you like to work with first?" (Notice he says "work with," not "look at.") By starting with *the buyer's* preference—not his own—

Tommy gets an order going within five minutes. And he *writes it down*.

Several hours later, the buyer leaves. By this time, Tommy has writer's cramp. He hasn't stopped! (I know. I've seen some of his orders. Wow!)

As I pointed out before, once a man has definitely committed himself to buy *something* from you, that's when it's easiest to get him to buy more.

And the pencil—our old friend the Magic Wand—sure helps.

Sales Memo from a Pro

One of the real Selling Aces at this multiple-line selling is Bill Brantman, head of Allied Western Distributors in San Francisco. Bill has built up a highly successful organization selling bar gadgets, kitchen novelties, and the like, throughout the West.

And, boy, does Bill know how to Deal in Diamonds! He makes every 50¢ item look like a million dollars!

Some time ago, Bill showed me a Sales Memo he sent out to his men. Because so much of it applies specifically to what we're talking about, I'd like to give you some of Bill's suggestions, just as he wrote them:

1. *In presenting a new item*, build up a little *suspense* before showing the item. Make them want to see it.

2. *Do not pressure on any one item.* If, after build-up and selling facts, the buyer is not interested, forget the item! By building up sales resistance on one item, you build resistance on everything. If you have later sold the buyer on something else (maybe two or three items) and he is thus in a buying mood, you can always come back with a pleasant: "Say, why don't you try a few of these, too!"

3. Spend less time with accounts on bull sessions. If you have nothing more vital to talk about than the weather, don't talk! Don't chit-chat *unless you have something to say*.

4. *Do not exaggerate* sales possibilities of an item. Telling an account they will sell six dozen in a month and then having

them sell only 36 will make them unhappy. And yet, selling 36 may be darn good; but the psychology was wrong.

5. Make *greater use of samples* on repeat calls. We always show samples the first time around, but do you remember when an account says "maybe next time" on an item on the first trip? Showing it again and again and telling them the sales possibilities and reorder sales you have had will wear them down politely but effectively. Please show it!

There!

The only Memo *I* can add to those suggestions is that I know they're good. They've sure paid off for Bill Brantman and his men.

Why not put 'em to work for you?

Chapter 21 in a Nutshell

1. If an item doesn't belong in the center ring, it doesn't belong in the line.
2. Write away—right away. Put each "yes" in black and white.
3. More suspense, more samples, more show, more sell— more sales.

Chapter 22

HOW TO KEEP YOUR
PRESENTATION FRESH

Canned or Planned—That Is the Question

Here's a debate that's been raging in sales circles since long before you or I came upon the scene. Just how precisely *should* your sales presentation be worked out in advance? Should you memorize your pitch word for word, or is it better simply to play it by ear?

As with most questions in selling, there is no *one* pat answer that fits all situations.

But I happen to have some pretty strong feelings on the subject—based on all the presentations I've watched over the years, good and bad—so I'll tell you how I feel about it. After all, right now, I'm doing the talking!

I say that *most* of the *best* sales presentations *are* doped out beforehand and delivered pretty much the same to *most* prospects *most* of the time.

This may seem to contradict some of what I've said before, so perhaps I'd better explain it.

I'm dead set against a strictly canned presentation—as I've said before. It's vital to get the prospect talking, to listen to what he says, and to proceed accordingly—as I've said before.

But—and this is the all-important point—only when you are

thoroughly prepared, only when your presentation is properly *planned* from start to finish, can you deliver your sales talk effectively.

Or—to put it another way—the only way to keep your presentation fresh is to make sure it isn't!

One of the most popular shows on TV right now is N.B.C.'s "Today" program. Why? Because the program always seems so spontaneous. And why is that? Because it isn't! Believe me, every detail is worked out meticulously in advance. And it's *because* of this thorough preparation that everyone can relax and behave with such apparent spontaneity.

I first found this out for myself the year after I got out of college. I had taken a fling at being a professional magician—a pretty successful fling, actually, besides which it was a lot of fun.

Anyway, another fellow and I were booked on a tour of schools throughout California. We worked up a sort of magical Abbott and Costello act for these shows, with all the tricks and gags meshed into a rather complicated routine of "Double Deception." We averaged about five shows a day, and, believe me, those kids provided plenty of audience participation, whether we wanted it or not!

Well, at the start of the tour, we found that every unexpected development became a real crisis. If the kids made too much noise, or if something happened to one of our gimmicks, we were in trouble.

But by the end of the first month, when we had put on the show a hundred times, we were *prepared* for anything. Because we knew what we were doing—and *knew* that we knew —nothing bothered us. If we got off our regular routine, it didn't matter, because we knew *how to get back on the track.* So we could *afford* to be spontaneous!

And it's the same way in selling. If you know your presentation—*really* know it—then you won't be afraid of tough situations, tough objections, or tough prospects. You'll know how to handle 'em all!

Then you can relax—and be spontaneous.

Every New Audience Is a New Show

I've made several references here to show business. If you're wondering what this has to do with selling, the answer is practically everything. Just as every line spoken by an actor is *planned* to portray a certain character in a certain situation, so it is that every word *you* speak must be planned to persuade the prospect to buy. You have to want that sale more than anything else in the world, without *seeming* to care at all! And, gentlemen, that requires acting.

Now, one of the first rules of show business—and it applies equally to selling—is that every new audience is a new show. No matter how many times *you've* heard that pitch of yours before, your prospect hasn't. To *him* it's brand new.

Therefore, in the last analysis, your presentation is *always* fresh. It *can't* get stale! If anything does get stale, it's you!

So what we're really talking about here is this: How can *you* stay fresh? After delivering the same pitch over and over, how can *you* make every performance sparkle like on opening night?

The best suggestion I can make is that you take a cue from my friend George Torrance, who is one of the most successful encyclopedia salesmen I've ever known. In his business, as you know, each man uses the same basic presentation, which is delivered almost word for word in home after home.

It's not easy to stay fresh under the pressures of a grind like that! But George does it, and here's how:

1. INTEREST. Everyone knows you have to develop interest on the part of the prospect. But how about the *salesman?* (No one talks much about that!) *You* have to be interested in this deal, too! In fact, if you're not interested—*sincerely* interested—sure as shootin', the prospect won't be.

So one of the best ways to stay fresh, according to George Torrance, is to be *interested*—really concerned—about your product, your prospect, and your presentation. Every time!

2. CONVICTION. Again, as I've said before, the prospect must

be convinced before he'll buy. And you? You have to be convinced and *convincing*. If you're an exceptionally fine actor, you might succeed in making the prospect believe something without truly believing it yourself. But few of us are that good.

For most of us, this has got to be a two-step process. First, you believe. Second, you inject this conviction into every word. With enough *conviction,* every presentation is new. Every time!

3. ENTHUSIASM. Ah, here's the one real miracle ingredient! With enough enthusiasm, mere mortals can work wonders! There's certainly nothing stale about a man who is truly enthused—about anything.

Bear in mind this is not the same as interest. You need both. You can be interested in a dead turtle without getting very enthusiastic about it. In selling, you have to be interested *and* enthused.

For some salesmen, this is the toughest of George Torrance's three points. We get enthused automatically, of course, over any exciting adventure that's new. Not when it's old hat.

But that's exactly why enthusiasm is so vitally important to a salesman. If you act really enthusiastic, it will *seem as though the whole proposition is brand new.* And that makes it fresh! Every time!

Those, then, are George Torrance's three points for keeping yourself fresh. I'd say they all make a lot of sense.

By the way, I don't know if you noticed that the initials of those points spell I-C-E. Maybe so—but by using them George has stayed hotter than a firecracker for years.

So can you.

Mastering the Prepared Ad-Lib

Well, we're back to show business—just for a little while.

For here is one of those little "tricks of the trade" that so many entertainers use to keep their presentations fresh. It should be equally helpful to you as a salesman. I know I've trained lots of men to use it, and it works.

It's simply a matter of stumbling on a word or a phrase—

just a little—to make it *seem* as if you're talking strictly off the cuff. But you're not!

Just like the actor in the TV soap opera who says: "Mary, the way you've been carrying on lately, I don't—I—I just don't know what to say!" He knows darn well what he's going to say! It's all in the script. But by hesitating that way, he gives us the *impression* that he's making it up as he goes along.

This is why the automobile salesman says: "When you touch your toe to the gas pedal, it's—it's—well, it's like taking off from Cape Kennedy!" Without that little hesitation, it might seem as if he'd *planned* to say that!

And this is why the business machine Ace says: "This new Error-Eliminator feature of ours is almost like—like—well, it's practically like having a silent sentry guarding every step of the work!" The *hesitation* makes it seem impromptu.

Try this technique yourself. It's good!

Just one word of caution.

As I said at the beginning of this chapter, you have to *know* what you're going to say. The prepared ad-lib is effective only when it's *prepared*.

Don't Be Afraid to Throw Out the Can

If you have to.

Now, this may seem to contradict everything I've been saying. But, as I've also said, in selling there are exceptions to every rule.

So no matter how perfectly you've prepared your presentation, no matter how much interest, conviction and enthusiasm you inject into the interview, and despite all your prepared ad-libs, occasionally there comes a time when you have to deviate.

And when that happens, your can (or plan) is worthless. Throw it out.

Earlier in this chapter, I mentioned encyclopedia salesman George Torrance, a real Selling Ace. But that business is like every other: there are some deuces and dunces along with the Aces.

A few years ago, when my daughter was entering high school, I decided we ought to get an encyclopedia. I called the nearest office of the ——— Encyclopedia. (All names will remain anonymous to protect the guilty.) I was a real live one.

A few days later a real sharp gal (or so she seemed) appeared at our door. We invited her in. She went through her pitch. We were interested. We were, in fact, about to buy.

Then, just before she finished her presentation, I asked to see something in one of the volumes. She said: "Sure, I'll be happy to have you look at the book, but right now I want to tell you about this . . ."

I asked if I might look at what I wanted to look at. (I wasn't throwing the kid a curve—honest. I *wanted* to see the darn thing, because I was interested.) She said: "Of course, naturally, look at it all you want. But right now," grabbing it away, "I want to show you this . . ."

P.S. We didn't buy the encyclopedia.

So prepare everything in advance, even your ad-libs. Get it all letter-perfect. Then use all the interest, conviction and enthusiasm you need to make it seem 100% off the cuff.

But—if you have to go off on a tack that *is* really new, do it. You're man enough!

And now, having gone through the guts of the presentation, you're also man enough to ask for the order.

Which we'll talk about in the next Part.

Chapter 22 in a Nutshell

1. Planned is good—canned is bad. There's a world of difference.
2. Don't worry about the presentation being fresh. Just make sure **you** are.
3. They've never heard it, so say it as if you'd never said it.
4. When it's time for a change, make it.

PART IV

Chapter 23

THE POWER OF POSITIVE SELLING

The First Decision is Yours

A salesman is a man who *closes* sales. Not a nice guy who drops in for periodic visits. Not a commercial tourist. By definition, any salesman worth his sample case is a man who persuades somebody to *buy*, not just to look or listen or think it over. To *buy*.

Obviously, this involves a *decision* on the part of the buyer, a decision which, in most cases, he wouldn't make without your help. (Otherwise, the company wouldn't need *you!*)

This means that *you* have to make a decision, too—the same decision you want *him* to make—and you have to make yours first. Right off the bat, you have to decide in your own mind that this fellow is going to buy.

And—most important—you have to *let him know* that you've made this decision.

Otherwise, you can be pretty sure, *he* won't make it.

Remember, nobody thinks any more of your proposition than you do. Confidence is contagious, but so is fear. If you act doubtful, so will the prospect. And doubt is something you can't tolerate at this point. You want that decision—*now*.

Way down deep, of course, you know that the prospect might *not* buy. But your every word and action must convey the idea that you *know* he *will*. As I've said before, selling takes acting. And right here you have to act *positively*.

During this entire Part we'll be talking about specific ways of getting the favorable decision you want and need.

But remember, the first decision is yours.

Persistence Pays Off

A moment ago I said that a salesman isn't a nice guy who drops in for periodic visits. Now I'll say something else: Sometimes a salesman isn't a nice guy at all! Not really.

If a prospect tells you he just plain doesn't want to buy, probably the *nicest* thing for you to do is pack up and leave. But that wouldn't be good selling. And, of course, you know in your heart that he'll be better off if he *does* buy, so you stay and sell. Even though, at the moment, it may not seem nice.

And if you do find yourself outside the door without an order (which, let's face it, happens sometimes, too) you go back and try again another time. Even though, at the moment, it may not seem nice.

Because—within reason—persistence pays off.

I remember a sales program we set up recently for Schlitz Beer. As is customary, it became my pleasant duty to introduce the plan at a sales meeting. When I had finished, Schlitz's New York Sales Manager, Stanley Feld, added a postscript:

"I just want you fellows to know," he said, "that this guy Wolfe practices what he preaches. When he first presented his plan to us, we threw him every curve in the book. But every time we came up with an objection to the idea, Wolfe gave us another reason why we should decide in favor of it. It took him three calls, but he kept selling until he got the order!"

Here's the point.

In most kinds of selling, both time and money are involved in every phase of the interview. Except in certain rare instances, the sale is apt to be a long process. Every time you Start with a Spade, Hit 'Em in the Heart, and Deal in Diamonds, you have an *invesiment* in that potential customer. Why not do everything possible to collect on it?

So if it takes a little more time and a little more effort, spend it.

It's usually a lot cheaper than starting all over again on somebody else.

The Customer Isn't Always Right

Every salesman is engaged in public relations—the public, in this case, being your customers. And there's no more important public relations job in the world.

For without good customer relations, you wouldn't have customers. Without customers, your company wouldn't have a business. And you wouldn't have a job.

So you tend to treat every buyer with kid gloves. The customer, they say, is always right. Competition being what it is, you probably want to do business with that fellow just a little more—if not a great deal more—than he seems to want to do business with you.

But the *best* salesman-buyer relationships are dedicated to the proposition that *both* men are created equal. The salesman makes it plain that any transaction will benefit *both* parties concerned. Hence, there is mutual respect on both sides. And there is a lot more business done.

Again, it's largely a matter of confidence on the part of the salesman.

In my own outfit, we do business with a lot of production people: printers, binders, film laboratories, recording studios, etc. Some of these folks seems so anxious to serve us that they'll promise anything, whether they can actually deliver the required job at the specified time or not.

But Ed Long, head of the Sales Promotion Essentials Corporation, is unique. On occasion, Ed has turned his place upside down to get our clients' work out on time. Whatever can be done, *is* done. We're the customer. But when something *can't* be done, he'll tell us that, too—and I respect him for it. Apparently, a lot of other people do, too, because S.P.E.C. is one of New York's most successful production operations. They certainly get the lion's share of *my* business.

So the next time a customer makes an unreasonable demand, or a prospect beats you down to where the sale stops being profitable, don't be a Casper Milquetoast. Stand up like a man, and say: "Look, Mr. Jones, this is what I can do and this is what I can't do." You'll get more respect from him—and more business.

This whole Part is about closing the sale. But there's no point in taking an order if you can't deliver, or if it isn't profitable. And the best way to make sure you don't get trapped into this kind of situation is to establish the right sort of mutually *respectful* relationship with every buyer.

It's all part of positive selling.

Chapter 23 in a Nutshell

1. Faint heart ne'er won fair lady—nor big order.
2. Don't be pigheaded about it—just determined.
3. The customer is always right unless he's wrong.

Chapter 24

CLOSING TECHNIQUES OF THE ACES

Ask the Man to Buy

This chapter is devoted to *successful* closing techniques. These are the methods that really work to clinch the close for many of America's top Selling Aces.

Some of them are simple and bald, others are artfully deceptive—but they're all *honest*. In print or otherwise, I won't have anything to do with any other kind. Even if you never have to face a buyer again, you still have to face yourself in the mirror. As far as I'm concerned, con games are out.

Especially since the simplest methods are often best.

So, to start with, here's the most direct closing technique ever devised: you simply *ask the man to buy*. So obvious, it sounds silly. Yet it's remarkable how many salesmen neglect asking for the order.

Several years ago, a fellow came around to sell us on exhibiting in the Sales Aids Show, to be held at the Hotel Biltmore in New York. He told us that here, for the first time, was a quick, inexpensive way for us to meet thousands of new prospects for our particular type of service—a real Heart-Appeal approach if I ever heard one! Then he went on to explain how the huge, yet select, attendance of top executives was assured, and he showed us a floor plan for the booths, to prove what an attractive layout had been designed, including red velvet drapes as a background for our exhibit. Boy, this fellow Dealt in Diamonds all the way! I was sold.

But then, as you've probably guessed, he forgot one thing —he didn't *ask me to buy*. So I didn't.

Fortunately—for us as well as for the show—the incident didn't end there. Tom Noble, Chairman of the Sales Aids Show, called me on the phone a few days later and wrapped up the deal. As a result, the show got our business, and we got several valuable new clients.

Why didn't Tom's salesman get the order? Simply because he didn't ask for it.

You've heard the story of the gorgeous, luscious debutante who married the ugliest, stupidest jerk in town. A friend asked her: "With all the handsome cavaliers you've known, why in Heaven's name did you latch on to *that* character?" The answer: "Because he *asked* me."

Orders are the same way. If you don't ask, you don't get.

So the next time you get into what we sometimes call "the saddle of the sale"—when the prospect is just plain cogitating and can't seem to make up his mind—just come right out and say: "Well, how about it, Mr. Jones, can I put you down for three dozen?"

You might be amazed. He's apt to say "Yes"!

As I said, this is not the cleverest closing technique in the world. Some will say it's no good at all.

But it's a whale of a lot better than not asking at all.

The Minor Decision Method

Those who dislike the direct-question close are usually hot for this one. According to some of my colleagues, the Minor Decision Method is foolproof.

With this system, you never put the question directly. Instead of asking *if* he wants to buy, you ask *which* he prefers: the red one or the black one, large or small, six dozen or a gross, today or tomorrow, parcel post or air freight, etc., etc. Whatever the answer, you've got yourself a deal.

Here's how it works.

The National Cash Register man, pitching a new luncheonette, says: "And *where* would you like us to install the register, Mr. Barnes, behind the fountain or over there by the door?"

According to the most eager proponents of this dodge, the poor guy *can't* say no! It's impossible.

That, of course, is downright silly. Let's face it, he *could* say: "Nuts to your cash register, I'll use a cigar box."

But, nevertheless, there is a psychological advantage here.

Perhaps the major drawback to the Minor Decision Method is its notoriety. Buyers know something about selling, too, you know. So if you're too obvious about it, you might get caught being too clever—and that wouldn't be clever of you at all.

But if you've never given this system a whirl, it might be worth a try.

When will you: on your next call, or the one after?

The Red Herring Switch

Now for a real piece of hanky-panky.

The Red Herring Switch is actually a good deal like the Minor Decision Method, except that here there is true art. Ah, how subtle!

In this case, you first manage to get the prospect's mind completely away from the act of buying, by injecting some more-or-less extraneous detail into the discussion—preferably a matter of importance to the customer, though not to you. Then you make a Big Thing of this extraneous detail—the Red Herring. Next, you let the prospect *sell you* on this other minor point. And finally you graciously give in and accept the deal on his terms—which is just what you had in mind all along.

If this sounds a trifle complicated, that's because it is. But it's worth mastering.

Let me give you an example.

We were once assigned the job of setting up a dealership sales program for the City Tank Corporation, manufacturers of the very fine and justifiably famous Roto-Pac garbage truck bodies, the kind with the "escalator" packing system on the back. Wherever City Tank had no dealers, we were to appoint them and help get them going.

In one major East Coast city, there was one particular firm that we felt would be best qualified to handle the line, and it became my job to "sell" this outfit on becoming the City Tank dealer in that area. A real sales job it was, too, because the deal involved an investment of approximately $20,000. And, naturally, that investment became the major question at issue. It seemed, in fact, like an insurmountable obstacle.

So I threw in the Red Herring. Instead of asking for the order, I told this firm that I didn't think I could accept the deal for my client unless they agreed to a smaller area than that which they normally covered. Naturally, this didn't go over too well. I didn't expect it to. So they started selling *me* on enlarging the territory back to what it probably should have been in the first place.

Finally, grudgingly, I accepted the $20,000 order!

Whether it's a question of specifications, delivery, discount, or whatever, you can usually find some Red Herring to throw into the conversation.

Let the other fellow concentrate on selling you on that point, and he'll often automatically sell himself on the whole deal.

If anybody wants to claim that much of the material in this book is pretty basic stuff, he can. It is. But he'll have to change his tune now.

The Red Herring Switch is a tricky and deceptive bit of sales strategy. It's for Aces only.

The Pencil Game

Back in the last Part we talked about using your pencil as a Magic Wand to help make a more forceful presentation. And it certainly works well in that role.

But your pencil can perform even greater miracles during the close. In fact, this is one of the simplest, yet one of the most effective, ways to clinch the sale.

With this method, all you do is *write the order before you actually get it!* After you've written it down, *then* you get the guy to approve what you've written! Does that sound a trifle daring? Definitely! But you'd be amazed how often it works.

One of the sharpest outfits around, in my opinion, is the Reuben H. Donnelley organization, selling agents for the telephone directory "Yellow Pages." Training Director Tom Pulliam has his team operating like a well-oiled Swiss watch, and he counts this closing technique as one of the strongest weapons in the Donnelley sales arsenal.

The Donnelley salesman carries a bunch of forms. He introduces them fairly early in the interview, usually referring to "your ad in last year's book." Nothing is said about "order blanks." While discussing a proposed ad, which the prospect has not yet agreed to buy, the salesman casually writes the details on one of these forms. Naturally, at the same time, he keeps talking. Then, just as casually, he slides the innocent-looking form in front of the prospect. The prospect signs—and the Donnelley Ace chalks up another sale.

Obviously, if the prospect is dead set against your proposition, this won't work. (Nor will any other closing method.) But when the decision you want is just hanging in the balance— as is so often the case—this clever little gimmick will many times provide the gentle push you need to Cushion 'Em with a Club.

Try it. The worst you can do is burn up a couple of extra order blanks.

Dotted Line Devices for Experts

Of course, the Pencil Game is useless unless the order gets signed. No closing method is worth a darn without a signature. When a name goes on that dotted line—*that's* when you've got the order. And not until.

Consequently, many salesmen get a slight case of epilepsy every time they face the crucial moment when the prospect signs—or doesn't sign—the order.

This, of course, is dead wrong. As I've said before, fear is contagious. If *you're* afraid of the deal, think of the prospect. He has to foot the bill!

So Rule #1 in asking for the signature is: *act nonchalant.* Figuratively speaking, snap your finger! This whole deal, it doesn't mean a thing!

Rule #2—a corollary to the first—is: *avoid the word "signature."* Never ask the prospect to "sign" the order. It sounds too forbidding. Instead, ask him to simply "O.K." it for you.

An even more subtle way to do it is to omit any mention of the signature at all. With this method, you just point to the dotted line and say: "All right, Mr. Jones, right here if you will please." (Note the absence of commas in that last phrase. That's the way you say it.)

Back in Part II, I mentioned a technique used by the International Correspondence Schools to develop a "yes" attitude during the approach. They're real Aces at getting names on dotted lines, too.

"Just put your name right here," the I.C.S. man explains, *"exactly as you want it to appear on the diploma!"*

Beautiful?

Or you can take a cue from Ace Toby Bickerstaff, who attended one of our Workshops in Houston. He simply remarks, casually: "Press hard. There are three copies!"

Ed Kudlich, head of Honolulu's fastest growing real estate and insurance firm, and one of my very closest friends there, worked out a cute gimmick. After writing up the deal, Ed lays his pen down crosswise on the contract, lifts up the edge nearest him, and lets the pen *roll* across the desk into the prospect's lap. Being a gentleman, the prospect *has* to pick it up. And there he is, ready to write.

And there *you* are, ready to try it yourself!

Of course, if you have to get your customer to sign a check, as well as the order, that's a little tougher. But the same principles apply.

Example:

I once considered buying an airplane from an outfit in Denver. Here, the salesman had the job of completing the sale —and a pretty big one, at that—by long distance telephone.

About the time he figured he had me sold, this fellow casually remarked: "Mr. Wolfe, why don't you just throw a $1000 check in the mail, and I'll hold it for you."

Get that! "*Throw*" $1000! He made it sound like knocking ashes off a cigarette!

As it finally turned out, I didn't buy the airplane—so maybe this is a poor example. But I don't think so. I think that closing sentence was a masterpiece.

As I said at the start, the whole secret is to *act nonchalant*.

The close is probably *the* most important part of the sale. Everything you say and do—and how you say and do it—has vital significance.

But you have to act as if you don't give a damn.

Chapter 24 in a Nutshell

1. Ask 'em to say "yes" or "no"—either is better than neither.
2. Ask 'em to say "yes" or "yes"—that's better yet.
3. Ever seen a red herring? Neither will the prospect when you use one.
4. The Pencil Game is fun. Everybody wins.
5. A lot of sales are started over a bottle of whiskey—but they're all closed over a bottle of ink.

Chapter 25

HOW TO APPLY LOW PRESSURE
WITH HIGH POWER

Strike While the Buyer Is Hot

Again, I want to emphasize my conviction that too much high pressure is bad. Strong-arm techniques usually make more enemies that sales. That's why we say, "*Cushion* 'Em with a Club."

But high *power* is a far different thing. High power, properly applied, makes it easy for you to close more sales *without* using undue pressure on the customer.

Just as a golf pro drives his ball twice as far as the duffer, with half the effort, so can the professional Selling Ace clinch more sales, more easily, by using the right techniques.

That's what this chapter is all about.

And the first rule here is: *strike while the buyer is hot.*

As we've discussed, and as you certainly know, there are several steps to making a sale. The reason, obviously, is that there are several steps to making a *purchase*. The buyer's mind has to go through several phases. The prospect may start out mildly interested, or even decidedly opposed. Then, if you do your job right, he starts getting hot. Usually, there's a period of wavering on his part—one moment he thinks "no," next moment he thinks "yes," another it's "no" again.

So, obviously, the easiest time to close him is at that instant when *he* is readiest to do business.

This is a prime reason for tuning in your "sales radar" as

described in Part III. This is how you determine when the guy is ready to be closed. You avoid hitting him over the head (even gently) before he's in a buying mood.

But when he *is* hot, you strike NOW. You don't wait for *anything*.

I remember when I started selling radio time in Honolulu. I was just out of college. I'd never read a book on selling—much less written one.

But one policy of the station seemed, even to my untrained eye, pretty silly. The salesmen used to go out and pitch the various potential accounts, sometimes for a few minutes, sometimes for months, before anybody agreed to a particular advertising schedule. Then, when an account was finally ready to do business, the salesman would go back to the station and *return later* with the contract ready to be signed! Hell, by that time the guy might have changed his mind, or the competition might have come along with another plan, or the brother-in-law might have talked him out of it—or anything else.

So I made it *my* policy to carry contracts with me. When I turned 'em in, they were written in longhand, rather than typed. Not nearly as pretty. But each one was signed by the buyer at the exact time when he most *wanted* to sign it!

Which may have been one reason why there were more of them.

Sell with an Automatic Transmission

When I say, "Strike while the buyer is hot," I don't mean strike *suddenly*.

This may seem like another paradox, so perhaps I'd better explain.

While the close should be timed as precisely as possible to coincide with the prospect's readiness to buy, it shouldn't come as a single, isolated knock-out punch. Above all, it mustn't be *announced*.

The idea is to *glide* into your close. Just as a smoothly operating automatic transmission shifts gears virtually unnoticed, so does the Selling Ace move into the close innocuously—because any sudden move on the part of the salesman causes a sudden barrier of resistance to be put up by the buyer.

So, again, this "automatic transmission selling" makes it easier for you to close more sales with less pressure on the buyer, and far less effort on your part.

This is why the Donnelley salesman, mentioned in the last chapter, introduces the order form *early* in the interview. The prospect has a chance to get used to it before he's asked to sign it.

It's also another reason why it's so important to "put the prospect in the picture" early in the sale, as described in Part III. When the prospect is able to see himself enjoying the benefits of the product, mentally he already owns it! Hence, it's much easier to get him to make his dream come true.

This is also why so many companies, in various fields, offer a "free trial."

When we sold Muzak in Hawaii, this free-trial gimmick clinched the majority of our sales. We, of course, were only too glad to make the gamble involved, because once a firm's employees got used to music on the job, the boss seldom had guts enough to order it removed!

The whole point is this.

If your closing attempt comes as a completely unexpected, sudden move—if it's accompanied by a big fanfare, like the circus drum roll announcing the triple somersault on the trapeze—the buyer is instantly put on guard. He immediately thinks to himself: "Aha! now he's going to try to sell me. I'll fix him!" And you're in trouble.

But if the close is made just an incidental part of the selling process, then the "low pressure with high power" is a pretty easy thing for you to apply.

And, like anything inevitable, the buyer just relaxes and enjoys it.

Let 'Em Cast Their Own Vote

During a recent national political convention, one of the candidates was accused of "rigging" the deal to prevent a fair and open contest. Personally, I doubt that this allegation could have been true under the circumstances, but the point is clear.

People like to cast their own votes. They don't like to be pressured.

Applied to selling, this means that people don't like to be sold. They want to *buy*.

So here we go again with another paradox.

To do an effective closing job, by definition, you have to help make the decision for the prospect. But you also have to *make him believe* that the decision is entirely his.

A neat trick if you can do it—and you can.

Essentially, there are two ways.

First, and most important, you simply *tell* the prospect that the decision must be his. Obviously, this has to sound 100 per cent sincere.

The encyclopedia salesman says: "I'd like to have your decision on this, Mr. and Mrs. Jones. After all, it's just as easy to say 'no' as it is to say 'yes'—it's strictly up to you how important your child's education is to you."

The sales engineer says: "About all I can do is explain why our equipment will save money and increase profits for you, Mr. Smith. The decision to take advantage of it has got to be yours."

The second way, already shown in these two examples, is to make it obvious to the prospect *which way* he should decide.

Which, of course, is again part of the over-all selling process.

Armchair Salesmanship

This high-power/low-pressure technique is similar to the above—only more so.

Here, you not only let the prospect feel that the decision is entirely his—you also let him know that maybe you wish he *wouldn't* buy!

That's why I call it "armchair" salesmanship. It's the lowest pressure, "I-don't-give-a-damn"-dest kind of selling in the world! But, brother, it packs a wallop.

Again, let me give you a couple of examples.

An obvious case is the automobile business.

Let's say you're driving a car worth, at today's used-car market value, $1500. (I don't know, maybe it's just your second car.) Anyway, it runs fairly well, but it will need some money spent on it pretty soon. It's certainly no cream-puff.

Then, one day, you see the car of your dreams sparkling in a showroom. It's tagged at $4250. You stop by just to look and drool.

An hour later, you have an offer of $2250 for your car, with easy payments stretched out so that you and your grandchildren can manage to pay off the balance of $2000 without too much trouble.

Then comes the clincher. The salesman points out a few of the deficiencies in your present buggy (which you know all about) and suggests that *maybe the boss won't accept the deal.*

That's when you decide you really want it!

Another example can be found in the way some computer systems Aces operate. Now, with today's modern technology, the tremendous advantages of electronic data processing are available to companies of almost any size. One of our fast growing clients, Computer Complex, Inc., even offers a "time-sharing" plan whereby a firm pays only for the computer time that is actually used—giving them the benefit of the Complex's highly sophisticated equipment, right at their fingertips, at a bare fraction of the cost that would otherwise be incurred.

But, because of the type of equipment involved, computers still carry a sort of "snob appeal" with many people. And the smart Selling Ace in that business can use this to his advantage.

Here's how the "armchair technique" can come into play.

The salesman says: "Mr. Jones, frankly, I'm not sure that your company qualifies for our service. After all, our equipment costs a lot of money. It was designed for the major blue-chips with highly technical problems to solve—and budgets to match. You may not be able to use this sort of thing in your business, and you may not be able to afford it. But if you really want to compete with the *leaders* in your industry . . . well, by golly, I'll see that installation is made right away. Now, all you have to do is okay this contract and . . ."

I made these examples fairly extreme—on purpose—and I want to hasten to add that they may not be typical. But I think you get the idea.

Naturally, I don't know to what extent, if at all, you can use this "armchair" technique in your own business.

But if you can use it, do so. Even if you have to tone it down a little.

It is actually—by far—the most high-powered low-pressure closing technique ever devised.

Chapter 25 in a Nutshell

1. There's a time for everything. The time for closing is NOW.
2. The smoother the shift, the surer the close.
3. If they're sold, they'll buy. And they'd rather.
4. The less you want to sell, the more they want to buy.

Chapter 26

THE EASY WAY TO HANDLE OBJECTIONS

Give the Enemy Credit

I'm referring again to the old Army rule: "Give the enemy credit for as much intelligence as you have." Essentially, it means that if you base your strategy on the hope that the other fellow will make a mistake, you'll probably end up fooling only yourself. The enemy is not apt to be a dope.

And this same axiom holds true in selling.

No prospect is ever likely to go along with *everything* you say. It just isn't normal for two humans to agree all the way on any proposition, especially when one man is paying money and the other is pocketing it.

So it's the rule—not the exception—for the buyer to object to something about your offer.

If you ignore the objection, it won't just go away. It will probably fester in the prospect's mind, and just when you think you've got your man sold, it will pop out like a boil to ruin the whole deal.

So, 99 times out of 100, objections *must* be answered—and they have to be answered *to the full satisfaction of the prospect*.

And, to do this successfully, you must first understand what the objection is, and recognize its validity. Because even when there's no true logic behind it, it's very real *to the prospect*.

And, in selling as in war, you have to give the enemy credit for having intelligence.

In this chapter, you'll see how Selling Aces answer these inevitable objections, to win sales instead of arguments.

That Marvelous "Yes-But" Gambit

This is the traditional way to answer most objections. Its one possible drawback—as with the "Minor Decision" close—is its reputation. Most buyers have heard it before.

But, of course, its popularity among salesmen stems from its merit. It has become a classic only because it's good. Used properly, it still works wonders.

Essentially, the "Yes-But" Gambit involves two simple steps: (1) you agree with the prospect; and (2) you offer evidence to counteract the objection. In other words, you make the positive outweigh the negative. You don't dispute the prospect's argument—you merely prove it isn't important.

The beauty of this technique is that you can use it with any product, tangible or intangible, and with virtually any objection.

Among Four Roses salesmen, for instance, the main complaint offered by the average liquor store owner concerns mark-up. "Give me the same discount I get on Old Underpants," the store owner says, "and I'll push your stuff like crazy."

The Four Roses Ace answers: "Sure, I know you get a longer mark-up on those off-brands." (Step #1.) "But with our national advertising, we guarantee you faster turnover, with far less effort on your part. All you have to do is display Four Roses—*we* sell it! At the end of the month, you're way ahead!" (Step #2.)

Years ago, when I was handling export sales for Mooney Aircraft, the only model offered was the Mooney Mite, a tiny single-seat craft. The stock objection was: "I don't like to fly alone." Our stock answer: "Neither do I! If I had my way about it, I'd take my wife along on every trip." (Step #1.) "But I *can't* take her, not in any airplane. She has to stay home with the kids! And most businessmen are the same way—however they travel, they usually travel alone. With the Mooney, you get the highest possible speed and performance, at the lowest possible cost!" (Step #2.)

Insurance men often hear this argument: "Hell, I'm only 30 years old! I don't think I'm going to die." And here's that good old "Yes-But" reply: "We don't *think* you're going to die either, Mr. Jones! That's why the premium at your age is so low." (Step #1.) "But none of us *knows* for sure. If we could foretell the future, we'd be millionaires and wouldn't need insurance! Life is uncertain, and life insurance is the one certain way to plan for that uncertainty!" (Step #2.)

And that's all there is to it.

First, you "give the enemy credit" by agreeing with him—wholeheartedly.

Second, you simply offer a plus that's stronger than the minus.

And the best part about the "Yes-But" Gambit is that it works even when the prospect is right!

The Great White Father Technique

But sometimes, of course, the prospect is just plain wrong. He raises an objection that simply isn't based on fact.

This *should* make it easier for you. When the guy is wrong, it ought to be a cinch to win the stupid jerk over to your side.

But it isn't!

Because when the prospect is off base, he can be *way* off base, so far off that no positive statement of yours can eliminate his negative. And still, you have to "give the enemy credit." You can't agree, you can't argue.

This is where you use the Great White Father Technique.

Again, there are two steps: (1) you admit that it's logical for the prospect to feel as he does; and (2) you show that somehow he must be mistaken.

You *don't* tell him he's wrong. You just prove it!

And, often, you help your cause by appearing totally amazed at this outcome!

Here are some examples as to how this works.

The industrial equipment salesman hears: "Your equipment

won't stand the gaff in my shop. I need something I can depend on." The prospect is wrong—it *will* stand up. So, using the Great White Father Technique, the salesman says: "I can understand how you feel, Mr. Jones, and, frankly, it's pretty hard to tell at first glance just how strongly this equipment is built." (Step #1.) "In fact, I was amazed, myself, when I saw these reports issued by Amalgamated Widgets. As you can see, they've been using our machines steadily on three shifts for over seven years without a single breakdown. With all of the cost-cutting features, you get solid, proved dependability!" (Step #2.)

The wholesale drug salesman has this thrown at him: "Everyone's asking for Brand X these days. I don't think your line will sell." To which the Selling Ace answers: "Certainly, sales are what you want and need, Mr. Smith, no doubt about that, and our line *is* new in this market." (Step #1.) "That's why we were pretty surprised, ourselves, when Schneider's sold three gross the first week, and Hoffman's Pharmacy just placed their fifth re-order this month. Yes, sir, it looks like our brand is really catching on!" (Step #2.)

I once bought a Piper Comanche airplane. (Now I fly a Twin Comanche—the greatest flying machine ever built. I've never seen such room, comfort and luxury in a light airplane—and it goes like the proverbial bat out of hell.)

Anyway, the distributor, Safair Flying Service, had one particular ship I wanted—with all sorts of super-duper radio equipment and other extras—but when I first test-flew the airplane, the air-speed indicator didn't show as much speed as I thought it should. "There must be something wrong with that airplane," I told Ted Hebert, boss of Safair. "It isn't as fast it ought to be."

Hebert—knowing I must be wrong—didn't argue. Instead, he said simply: "Well, if the airplane isn't right, we certainly won't sell it to you. Let's find out."

He arranged for a test. By flying the airplane alongside another one (which I had already checked and found O.K.) we discovered that the instrument was at fault—the airplane was fine. So the instrument was adjusted, I took delivery of the Comanche I wanted, and I'm as happy as a kid with a new toy.

So Ted Hebert—aside from being a fine gentleman and a seller of mighty fine airplanes—is also a master of the Great White Father Technique!

Here's the moral:

When the prospect is wrong, the "Yes-But" Gambit won't work.

The Great White Father Technique will.

The Inquiring Reporter

At the beginning of this chapter, I said that most objections have to be answered, because most objections are real—real, at least, in the sense that the prospect *believes* them to be valid and important. And so we've looked at effective ways to answer them.

But sometimes you sense that the prospect is simply throwing up a smoke-screen. This is when the objection just doesn't make sense. Somehow, you realize that even *he* doesn't believe what he's saying. You smell a rat.

In such cases, your best bet is to take the role of the Inquiring Reporter, to find out what (if anything) the prospect *really* has on his mind.

Because if the objection *isn't* real, either: (1) you can't answer it; or (2) even if you do, you're still nowhere, because there may be another, as yet unexpressed, objection which you don't know about.

So, putting your prospect in the glare of the spotlight, you start questioning. Mostly, you ask "why."

Again, here are some examples—necessarily vague, because objections of this kind come from so far out in left field.

The prospect says: "We're not quite ready for it. We'll let you know when we are." What does he mean? Is there a logical reason for waiting, or does he need approval from his brother-in-law? You have to find out. So you ask *why* he isn't ready.

Or he says this: "I don't think I want to do business with

your firm." Now, what does *that* mean? Was he mistreated by your outfit in the past? If so, how? Or has he heard vicious rumors? Again, you need facts. So you ask *why*.

Or this: "Sure, I know we ought to carry your line, but I'm sorry—the answer is no." Now, *there's* a mystery! If he knows he ought to carry it, why doesn't he? Is the other salesman making time with the boss's daughter? Is somebody getting a payoff? You'd better find out.

Naturally, you can get into some ticklish situations here. You've got to be as tactful and diplomatic as possible. But you still have to probe. Otherwise, you'll never sell the guy.

If you're clever at it, either one of two things will happen: (1) you'll uncover the *true* objection, and once it's unveiled you can answer it; or (2) the prospect will realize the fallacy of his argument, and talk himself out of it.

Unreal objections are the hardest to answer.

That's why you have to be an Inquiring Reporter.

Taking the "Ice" out of Price

As we saw in Part II, "Treasure" is a strong Heart-Appeal. Everyone likes to save money, and the fellow with a lower price has a definite advantage.

But, as pointed out in Part III, everyone wants quality, too. Although, obviously, you can't always have both.

Frankly, I'd much rather sell a *good* product than a cheap one. Without having to worry about every nickel and dime, you're far more secure. With high-end merchandise, certainly, you have a lot more to talk about. There's nothing better than the best.

But, since price *is* such a factor in today's economy—and I guess it always has been—let's take this up separately.

First of all, if your stuff costs more than the other fellow's it must be better. (If it isn't, you'd better get yourself a job with the competition.) You offer more quality features, heavier advertising support, faster service, or something else that's exclusively yours—*something* that the prospect can't get at the lower price.

So you point this out. You emphasize the fact that your quality is more important than the other fellow's price. (And it is—it lasts longer.) You show that product satisfaction always outweighs—and outlives—any minor saving. Not necessarily in these words, you make it plain that "you get what you pay for."

Most important, of course, you prove *why* yours costs more. You *justify* the price.

But if all of this doesn't work—if the prospect still balks—there's one favorite technique the Selling Aces use. It's another one of those high-power yet low-pressure methods—and I've seen it work miracles.

Once again, there are two steps: (1) you tell the guy to go ahead and buy the cheaper product; but (2) *you vigorously advise him to insist on the qualities you know he can't get with it!*

And, happily again, this technique works with anything.

"That's perfectly O.K. with me," you say. "Go ahead and place your order with them. But, because I know this one factor is so extremely important to you, just make sure you get . . ." (Mentioning whatever it is he *can't* get from anyone but you.)

This is a sly gimmick—and, hence, must be used slyly. It can't be too obvious.

But it's one of the cleverest ways I know to solve one of the biggest problems in selling. Master this one, and you'll really be able to Cushion 'Em with a Club!

Chapter 26 in a Nutshell

1. Objections need not be objectionable—"no" is natural.
2. When you accentuate the positive, you eliminate the negative.
3. The prospect may argue with you—he can't with the Great White Father.
4. Be an Inquiring Reporter. Plenty of "why's" will make you wise.
5. Let 'em buy it cheaper. Defy 'em to buy it better.

Chapter 27

THE MAN WHO WANTS
TO THINK IT OVER

Close Isn't Closed

Have you ever heard this one?

The salesman made a beautiful presentation. He did every-thing right—up to and including the close. The buyer said: "It looks good—but I'll have to think it over. Try me again next month." The salesman smiled. "That's O.K., sir, I wish I had 100 like you."

Next month the salesman returned, and went through the same pitch. The buyer said: "Gee, son, I'd like to give you an order—but I'll have to think it over. Try me again next month." The salesman was undismayed. "That's O.K., sir, I wish I had 100 like you."

And so it went, on and on, every time the salesman called.

Finally, the buyer had to ask: "Look. You've been calling on me for seven months. I've never given you a dime's worth of business. And still, you keep saying you wish you had 100 like me. Why?"

"Brother, I've got 1000 like you!"

Probably you *have* heard it, because that story has become a classic in sales circles. And the reason for that, obviously, is that it's so sadly typical. No matter what you're selling, all too often the buyer "wants to think it over." No reason—he just doesn't want to buy *now*.

And so perhaps a special chapter on this perennial problem might be worthwhile.

Especially since too many salesmen spend too much time kidding themselves, counting their orders before they're hatched.

In selling—as in most other fields of endeavor—almost is not good enough. In fact, the guy who boots you the hell out of the door is probably a better friend than the S.O.B. who keeps you dangling and hoping. He certainly puts just as many shekels in your pocket—and wastes a lot less of your time.

So the next time a buyer says: "Don't worry. I'm sure it's O.K. I just have to check on . . ." Follow his advice. Don't worry. But don't figure you've made a sale, either. Because you haven't.

Here are some of the methods Selling Aces use to land the fishes that would otherwise get away.

Settle for a Crumb

Back in Part III, we spent a whole chapter discussing ways to sell up—to make orders bigger rather than smaller. Certainly, that's what we all want.

But right here, we're not concerned with the *size* of the order. We're concerned only with the order itself—whether you get it or whether you don't.

And Rule #1 is: Take the order—*any* order. Anything is better than nothing.

As long as the buyer remains just a prospect, you remain just another peddler trying to get your foot in the door. You're strictly from nowhere.

But the minute business is actually transacted, everything changes. Now you're a supplier—a source—and the buyer is *your customer*. What a difference!

Tom Nast, President of All-State Welding Alloys, told me recently:

"We've cracked many of the leading firms in the country, and now we're an important factor to most of them. We get volume from these big accounts—and, of course, that's why we're successful. But, in virtually every case, we had to get our foot in the door first. We tell our salesmen to accept any order—no matter how small—if the account offers future potential."

And I think that's pretty good advice for almost any salesman.

So the next time a prospective buyer refuses to take a gross, get him to take a dozen. If he won't take a dozen, get him to take 1/12 of a dozen—assorted—if you have to. Anything to get that account on the books.

Because the only way to build an account is with business. Not with a promise to "think it over."

The Strategic Retreat Technique

Of course, the foregoing applies only to salesmen who have a *line* of products to sell, or a product where the quantity can vary. If you're selling a specialty item on a one-to-a-customer basis—one deal and that's it—obviously, you can't settle for less.

That makes the problem of the man who wants to think it over even tougher.

Here's a solution for you.

Again, it's a two-step process: (1) you appear to accept defeat gracefully, even start to leave; then (2) you swing right back into the sale.

This accomplishes three things.

First, by starting to retreat, you lower the buyer's resistance. Instead of maintaining that brick wall in front of you, he relaxes. He thinks he's won, so he stops fighting.

Second, you clear the air. The whole atmosphere of the office changes. You and the buyer are buddies again.

Third—and most important—you give yourself a whole new chance at the order. You can start right from the beginning— or from wherever you want—and begin to sell all over again.

Another company we've worked with is Executone, the intercom people. Here's how we trained their men to use the Strategic Retreat:

After the Executone Ace has completed his presentation—and he has plenty to present—if the buyer still wants to think it over, he says: "That's perfectly all right, Mr. Jones, no one could ask for a nicer reception than you've given me this morning!" And he starts to put away his portfolio.

But then, just as both men are rising from their chairs to shake hands cordially, the Ace stops and says, smilingly: "You know, before I leave, Mr. Jones, I merely want to show you *one* more thing about our equipment, something that should be mighty important to you. I just know you're going to be impressed with this . . ."

And off he goes again—in the direction of the order.

As I said at the beginning of this Part, persistence pays off—especially if you don't *appear* to be too persistent.

The Strategic Retreat Technique makes that possible.

Always Keep a Trump Up Your Sleeve

The Strategic Retreat Technique, as explained, gives you an opportunity to start selling all over again. This is a tremendous advantage, even if you have nothing concrete to add to what you've already said. The repetition alone may do the trick.

But your renewed selling efforts will be far more effective if you can throw in some extra clincher. Obviously, that's possible only if you have *saved* some reserve ammunition for this purpose.

And that's why it's smart to keep a trump up your sleeve—held until the very end when you need it most.

Some companies offer a cooperative advertising deal as a clincher—if they have to.

Other firms agree to a change in specifications—if they have to.

In other cases, the "trump" is purely and simply a price adjustment.

I've already mentioned the job I had many years ago in San Francisco, selling a radio promotional program over the telephone. The standard deal was $39.50, for which the account eventually received 300 "albums" around which the program was built. But, in radio terms, the point stressed was the six weeks' duration of the program.

If all other attempts to close failed, the pitch was: "I'm so sure you'll get benefit from this program, Mr. Jones, I'm going to let you try it for three weeks—at just half the cost, $19.75. Then, at the end of that time, you be the judge as to whether you want to go along for the remaining three weeks. Fair enough?"

Actually, this was a pretty sneaky dodge. The timing— three weeks vs. six weeks—had nothing to do with it, inasmuch as the guy's name was never mentioned over the air, anyway. For the $19.75 he simply got half as many albums.

A leading encyclopedia practices another piece of hanky-panky.

After all other Strategic Retreats and countercharges have been expended, the salesman says: "Say, I have an idea! I can't promise anything, but maybe . . . can I use your phone a moment?" Naturally, the prospect usually says O.K.

Then, the one end of the phone conversation (the only end the prospect can hear) goes like this: "Hello, this is So-and-so, may I please speak to Joe in the warehouse? Hello, Joe? Say, you know that one set we had in the trade show? Yes, that's the one. Is it still there? It is? Oh, that's wonderful! Mr. and Mrs. Snodgrass will be so happy! Hold it there—don't let it out of your sight!"

And finally, the salesman returns joyfully, and explains that this *one* set—because it was in the trade show, even though it is brand new—can become the proud possession of the Snodgrass family for even less than the regular low price.

Those, of course, are just a couple of examples. Being a salesman, yourself, maybe they appear too bald to be practical. But I can assure you that they do work successfully—and, naturally, I chose those two rather extreme cases strictly to illustrate the principle.

The exact nature of your "trump up the sleeve" isn't vitally important to the success of your sales effort.

But it *is* necessary to give the prospect a *reason* for buying *now*—otherwise, he probably won't.

He'll just "think it over."

Chapter 27 in a Nutshell

1. A deal isn't a deal until it's a deal.
2. Settle for a crumb if you have to—half a loaf is sometimes a lot.
3. Start to retreat—then start to sell all over again.
4. Keep your last trump until you play it to win.

Chapter 28

IF YOU CAN'T CLOSE THE SALE, DON'T CLOSE THE DOOR

You Can't Sell Everybody

This is probably the most unusual chapter ever written on selling. For this has to do with *not* making the sale. Here, mixed right in with all these sure-fire closing methods that *ought* to guarantee success every time, I want to talk about the procedures you should follow when the guy *doesn't* buy.

For let's face it—no selling technique works *all* the time, and nobody bats 1000. You can't sell everybody.

Now, according to legend, all good salesmen are born with thick skins. Promises can be broken, insults can be thrown, doors can be slammed—nothing ever bothers *them*. Salesmen are tough.

Well, don't you believe it!

Sure, as we all know, these things do happen, and a Casper Milquetoast type of personality is not recommended.

But, at the same time, the only folks who are wholly insensitive to others are morons—and morons make lousy salesmen. A good salesmen *must* be able to read the attitude of his prospect and react accordingly. And when that attitude is distinctly negative, this is bound to have an effect on any salesman's feelings.

So if occasional unkind words make you feel bad, don't let the fact that you *do* feel bad make you feel worse. You're only human—and what's wrong with that?

But there is a cure, and it's an important factor in your success as a Selling Ace.

It's simply the realization that *nobody* sells everybody.

You may have the greatest product in the world, your prospect may have the greatest need, and still it's just *possible* that he may not buy! No reason. He simply doesn't want it. Some folks just aren't hep.

I've met people who were opposed to Brigitte Bardot.

How to Tell When No Means NO

As I've said, you can't sell everybody. Despite *some* of the stuff you read on selling, there's no such thing as an infallible system, no panacea for all problems.

Sometimes no means NO.

At that point, any further selling efforts on your part would be futile, causing you, at best, to waste more time and money. Or, at worst, further pressure might completely ruin any future chances of getting business from the guy.

Persistence pays off. Being a pest doesn't.

Therefore, it's important to determine whether the "no" you hear is final, and why. As I see it, there are three types of "impossible" situations:

1. *When the buyer needs more facts.* This, of course, is apt to be your fault. Maybe you didn't have all the information about your proposition that you should have. Or maybe further specifications are needed, before the buyer can make an intelligent (and favorable) decision.

Obviously, this isn't an entirely hopeless (for the future) situation. Go get the facts and bring them back.

Maybe next time you'll be able to answer *all* the questions —and have better luck.

2. *When delay is destined.* Sometimes postponement can't be prevented. Maybe you didn't get in to see the right man. Possibly there are budget limitations that force a deferment of the decision. Or perhaps there's a temporary inventory situation which you can't do anything about. Or any one of a zillion other things.

As we've discussed, a promise to "think it over" or to "check on it" doesn't buy any groceries for you today. Still, there's hope.

Find out *specifically* what has to happen before you can get the order, and exactly *when* you can expect definite word.

Then *don't wait* for that word. Call back at the appropriate time.

3. *When the guy just isn't sold.* This is undoubtedly the most nearly hopeless situation of all. Notice I said "nearly" hopeless—because virtually any sale can be made if you work at it long enough and hard enough.

The important decision for you to make in this case is how badly you want this man's business. Certainly, anyone is worth a couple of call-backs. In some fields of selling, some customers are worth cultivating for years, if necessary, in order to get your foot in the door.

This is something you have to determine for yourself, depending on the kind of selling you do, and the potential value of the specific account.

Lose the Sale—Keep the Friend

We were just talking about the obvious fact that some customers are worth more than others. Also, the importance of any individual customer will vary greatly depending on the type of selling involved.

To an advertising agency, for instance, a new account may represent many millions of dollars in billings. To the average manufacturer's salesman, a steady customer can easily mean many thousands over the years. While to a specialty salesman, working on a one-shot type of deal, each customer may not, by himself, be very important at all.

So this is bound to affect any salesman's attitude toward the man who doesn't buy the first time around. And so it should.

But, contrary to some schools of thought among the high-pressure boys, I happen to believe that *every* potential customer is important to *every* salesman. There is *never* a situation when today's sale is more important than tomorrow's good-will. Or, if it is, you're in the wrong business.

It just doesn't pay to alienate anyone.

Therefore, no matter what you sell, or to whom—and regardless of the monetary value you place on any customer's head—when the final "no" is heard, *always* do these three things:

1. *Smile.* Maybe you can't be happy—but, at least, you can avoid getting mad. Your general attitude may have a lot to do with your chances at selling the guy next time. And, whether he ever buys or not, it may also count with his friends. So make your last impression a good one.

A line I like to use is: "Well, if we can't do business, at least we can be friends." And it pays off.

2. *Thank him for his courtesy.* I'm assuming that you received some. With a reasonable proposition and a decent approach, you nearly always do. Let the man know that you appreciate the time he has given you. After all, no matter how valuable your product, or how profitable your proposition, *you* are trying to sell *him*—not the other way around.

I've already mentioned the Executone Aces' favorite parting remark: "Thank you, Mr. Jones. No one could have asked for a nicer reception!" Like everyone else, they sometimes miss a sale. But I've rarely seen them leave without making a friend.

3. *Open the door for the future.* Never admit that all is lost forever (even when you feel it is). Nor do you want to make the mistake of saying something like: "I'll get you next time!" Both extremes are bad.

At this point, your non-customer must be looked upon strictly as a future prospect—no more, no less—and treated as such. Therefore, don't blame him for his refusal to buy, and don't blame yourself too severely for your failure to make the sale. If both parties are let off the hook, your chances for the future are much brighter.

The exact statement you make must depend, necessarily, on the specific situation—on the buyer's reasons for not buying.

But the all-important principle is this:

As I pointed out way back in Part II, each new call is a

new sales opportunity. Now is the time to open the door for that call, to make way for that opportunity.

Tomorrow's Another Day

We have now completed every phase of the sale, from beginning to end.

You have, I hope, picked up lots of valuable tips from the four Selling Aces:

> START WITH A SPADE
> HIT 'EM IN THE HEART
> DEAL IN DIAMONDS
> CUSHION 'EM WITH A CLUB

And you have even gotten some ideas, in this chapter, on what to do when these Selling Aces *don't* turn the trick.

Which brings us to the main point of this chapter, which is: *tomorrow's another day*. The success of that tomorrow depends on YOU.

And that is the one real Joker in the whole deal, which we'll cover in the last Part.

Chapter 28 in a Nutshell

1. Sell enough somebodies, and you don't have to sell everybody.
2. Learn to know when no means NO—then you'll know what to do about it.
3. You can't always make a sale—but you can always make a friend.
4. The brightness of your tomorrow depends on you today.

PART V

Chapter 29

DON'T FORGET THE "MAN" IN SALESMANSHIP

What You See in the Mirror

This will be the smallest Part of the book.

Yet it's probably the most important.

Because none of these selling techniques—*none* of them—mean a darn by themselves. Nor do any other sales ideas you will ever see or hear. They don't just happen. Selling never takes place in a vacuum.

Selling is a *human* experience. A sale is made only between *people*. Just as every sale of every product is made *to* an individual human being—as we discussed back in Part II—so is it also made *by* an individual human being. And that person is the *salesman*—in this case, YOU.

That's why the "man" in salesmanship is so vital.

Now, depending on the kind of selling that you do, as we have discussed, you may get to know your customers pretty well—which means, of course, that they get to know all about you, too. So, as they say, the "whole man" is important.

But not at the start. Not when you first walk in.

The first impression (and you know how lasting that can be) is *visual*. The buyer *sees* you before he hears you utter a word, and before he has a chance to judge you any other way. The sale can be made or lost—in part, anyway—right then and there.

That's why so many smart sales organizations keep a full-length mirror by the door. Every time a salesman goes out to sell, he *sees* himself as his customers will. If he looks wholly presentable, that fact gives him added confidence. If he doesn't, there's usually a place around the hall to do something about it.

Obviously, I'm not talking about the shape of your nose, the strength of your jaw, or the position of your hairline. Whether you happen to look like Rock Hudson or Lassie need not have any bearing on your success as a salesman—and, either way, you probably couldn't do very much about it. No, this has nothing to do with innate good looks.

It has to do, instead, with your *appearance*—and that you *can* do something about.

It's impossible to be specific about this, of course, because standards vary so greatly depending on the business and the territory. In New York, for instance, a business suit is the strict rule; in Hollywood a casual sport coat is perfectly O.K.; in Honolulu some fellows get by with aloha shirts.

As far as clothing goes, I think my college public speaking professor expressed it pretty well: "Dress at least as formally as the best-dressed man in your audience."

As a salesman, you should dress at least as well as your customers.

Even more crucial is *neatness*—your hair, finger nails, shoeshine, shave, etc. These are all pretty obvious, but you can't dispute their importance.

I remember a magician I once saw at an exclusive supper club in San Francisco. He came out looking like an ad in *Esquire:* white tie, tails, silk top hat, gold-tipped black cane— the works. Boy, was he suave!

Then, just as he got to the center of the floor, someone started tittering. A moment later there were more giggles from the audience. Soon everyone was laughing uproariously—while, needless to say, the performer became more and more confused.

It needn't have happened.

If that dapper magician had just looked in the mirror first— he'd have seen his fly was open!

What do *you* see when you look in the mirror?

The answer can well determine—and to a very great extent—your success as a salesman.

Beneath the Frosting

As I said a moment ago, the first impression you make on any prospect is visual. All you have to do is *look* O.K. and you pass the initial test, regardless of anything else.

But long before you get an order—and even longer before you ever get any repeat business—the buyer has a chance to learn some other things about you, too. And these things count for even more.

These are the factors that add up to what we call *personality*.

This is another thing you *can* do something about. It's *not* something you're born with. A man's personality—good or bad —is something that's *developed* over the years.

And don't let anyone kid you about the importance of it.

Sure, if one product is far superior to another, the average customer will buy the better item—regardless of the salesman's personality. If a similar product is available from one source at lower cost than from another, the buyer may take advantage of that saving—regardless of the salesman's personality.

I remember buying a car shortly after World War II, when cars were mighty hard to come by. The man who sold it to me was one of the most disagreeable individuals I've ever met. And still I bought—because I *needed* transportation.

But those are all rare, abnormal situations.

Your product is almost certainly *not* far superior to others. Your price is *not* apt to be much lower than the next fellow's. Your company does *not* have a monopoly on engineering genius. Thanks to the American competitive system, it's highly unlikely that anyone *has* to buy from you.

And, that being the case, the average customer will buy from the man he *wants* to do business with. The fellow he *likes* personally.

Which, again, is why the "man" in salesmanship is so important.

It pays to be a nice guy.

So You Want to Be an Extrovert

A generation or so ago, words like "extrovert" and "introvert" were found only in scientific journals. Today, during our present age of beatniks and headshrinkers, these are common terms. So it should be O.K. to use them.

The trouble is: their meanings are so often misunderstood. The true facts may come to you as a pleasant surprise.

Everyone knows that extroverts make the best salesmen—and this is true. But many people do *not* know which people make the best extroverts!

So let's get it straight.

By definition—and I'm getting this right out of *Webster's Dictionary*—an extrovert is "one whose interests lie mainly in external objects" and an introvert is "one who is preoccupied with his own thoughts, emotions, and motives." The important factor, you see, is *interest*.

An extrovert, therefore, does *not* have to be a lusty, back-slapping good-time-Charlie. He does not have to tell funny stories, nor be the life of the party. In fact, whenever a guy seems determined to be the star attraction, you can be pretty sure he's not as much of an extrovert as he'd like to think.

To be an extrovert, the only requirement is to be *interested in other people* and other things. That's what counts.

And this, again, is a faculty you can develop. It's just a case of putting your mind to it.

So the next time you greet a customer with, "How are you?" act as though you expect an answer. *Think* about it, and about the fellow you're talking to. Even if it makes you forget part of your sales pitch! Then, if the guy says, "I feel great! My boy just won a Scrabble scholarship to Harvard!" think about that, too. Remember it. Then, the next time you see that customer, you can show *interest* in him by making an appropriate comment regarding the son.

Remember, the important thing about personality is not exactly what you say, nor even precisely how you say it. The only thing that really matters is what you think and how you feel *about other people.*

If all you ever think about is *your* product, *your* order, *your* commission—YOU—then you're an introvert. And probably not a very good salesman.

Change that viewpoint, and you're an extrovert.

Will Rogers became an American legend when he said: "I never met a man I didn't like."

Because of that philosophy, everyone loved Will Rogers.

And that's why he was a real Selling Ace.

Chapter 29 in a Nutshell

1. What you see in the mirror is what others see first in you.
2. Personalities are not born, they're made. You'd better make a good one.
3. When you're interested in others, others are interested in you.

Chapter 30

WIDEN THE DOOR TO YOUR MIND

Knowledge Is Power

Throughout the book, I think I've made it pretty plain that product knowledge isn't enough—it's what you *do* with that knowledge that counts. Just as sales know-how isn't any help to you unless you remember the Joker—and *do* something about it.

Still, without knowledge you're lost. If knowledge isn't power, it's at least a darn good source.

Therefore, it's a smart idea to get all the know-how you can, about every phase of your business, and to get it *whenever* and *wherever* you can.

1. *Product and industry knowledge.* Every line of business has its trade publications. Read them. Not during your selling time—because that's too precious—but at home. If the boss won't let you take 'em out of the office, subscribe to a couple yourself. It's worth it.

And aside from current developments, as found in most trade magazines, every product has its own unique romantic history.

I recently had the pleasure of addressing a meeting of the National Pretzel Bakers Institute. Pretzels! There's a product most of us consider about as lifeless as any! Yet, through reading some of the Institute's material, you find that there's really quite a story behind the great American pretzel. Frank Tisdale,

Executive Secretary of the Institute, told me that the Selling Aces in that field know the story backwards and forwards—and *tell* it to their customers.

The Schlitz Brewing Company, another of our clients, prides itself on selling a *quality* beer. But what actually provides this quality? Why is one brand of beer better than another? Frankly, as the folks at Schlitz told me, some of their own salesmen don't really know. But the smart ones do. That's why they're smart—and successful.

2. *Sales know-how.* You can never learn too much about selling, either. So if a regular sales course is offered in your city, take it. I've seen many, some better than others, but I've never seen a bad one. When a Sales Executives Club, or some other organization, sponsors a short Sales Clinic, enroll in it. Again, some of these are more worthwhile than others—and, inasmuch as I'm one of the guys in that business, I can't be exactly impartial in my judgment. But you're bound to get *something* out of every affair of this kind that you attend.

Of course, the fact that you're reading this book indicates a desire to sharpen up. And, certainly, I approve of *this* activity!

Learning all you can about your own business, as well as about selling, will accomplish two things for you: (1) you'll become the kind of M.D. I spoke about in the very first chapter, so that you'll earn more respect from your customers; and (2) the boss is bound to notice, and that won't hurt you at all.

Don't Be a Worry Wreck

Talking about "widening the door to your mind," this might be a good time to mention the importance of keeping that door *open*. If your mind is clogged with other problems, you certainly can't concentrate properly on anything that pertains to your one prime job—which is, of course, selling. The man who is free to think is also free to sell.

Or, to put it another way, stay happy.

This is not a book on human relations, as such, nor do I claim to be in any sense a psychiatrist. But I've seen too many happy, successful salesmen—and too many *un*happy, *un*success-ful salesmen—not to know that there's a correlation.

A recent survey in *Fortune* pointed out an ever-increasing policy among smart business firms: they scrupulously interview the wife, as well as the man, when hiring salesmen. They want to know about the applicant's home life—along with his business life—because they know that the two can never be completely separated. Nor does the average company want them to be.

The next time you go looking for a job, you might keep that in mind.

Meanwhile—for your own sake, not your company's—you'd be wise to keep your home life as happy and serene as you can. And if the other members of your family realize how important this can be to the general welfare, they'll cooperate—assuming, of course, you're not a totally impossible guy to live with.

This applies to any other personal problems, too. Don't fret over them—solve them.

If your car doesn't run, get it fixed.

If drinking becomes a problem, cut it out.

If your tooth aches, see a dentist.

All of this is so obvious, you may think it silly. But the point is valid—and vital.

As long as your mind is bothered with *any* extraneous problems, you can't be fully effective in your job. Wipe out those problems, and you face a whole new world of selling success.

And if your job is the thing that you find unbearable, get another one.

Stand on Alert

Back in Part I, I said that "prospects are where you find them." Now I'd like to add something to that: Prospects are also *when* you find them. You just never know when a red-hot selling opportunity may turn up.

Which is why Selling Aces are *always* or. the look-out.

In our own Selling Aces Workshop classes, the fellows often turn new acquaintances into valuable customers. In one group in Houston, a realtor sold a home, an advertising agency executive landed a new account, a car salesman delivered two automobiles, a health studio representative signed up three enrollments, and a restaurant equipment salesman sold me a bar for our patio at home!

As a personal example, I do remember one of my Muzak experiences in Honolulu many years ago. My target was the Home Insurance Company, one of Hawaii's leading firms. I knew that if I got them, others would fall in line. The problem was to get close enough to the right man—a problem, incidentally, which had gone unsolved for several years.

Then, at a party one night at Honolulu's exclusive Pacific Club, I found myself right smack beside Home's bigwig boss. Where? In the men's room!

P.S. We signed 'em up the following week.

So keep the door to your mind open all of the time.

You'll find it's also the door to your order book.

Chapter 30 in a Nutshell

1. Widen the door to your mind—and let the knowledge pour in.
2. Stay happy and you'll stay hot.
3. Prospects are when you find them—if you want to.

Chapter 31

HOW TO BUILD A POPULAR
PERSONAL IMAGE

You're Always Selling

In this era of TV, international politics, and public relations, we hear a lot about "images"—the mental pictures that come to mind when we think of certain individuals. Normally, of course, the term is used in connection with famous celebrities.

But *you* represent an image, too—we all do within our own bailiwicks. The people who know you—and those who only know *of* you—all have an opinion about you, good or bad, which *you* have created.

And, as a salesman, it naturally behooves you to build the most popular personal image possible.

The first thing to remember is that *you're always selling*. Even when you're not trying. Even when the situation has nothing whatever to do with your job. *Everything* you say or do contributes to the over-all image.

Among non-celebrities, one of the most popular men I ever knew was my Uncle Larry. He's been dead for twenty years, but around Honolulu—and in several other parts of the world, too, for that matter—his image still lives.

Not because he was a tremendously kind-hearted and civic-minded man—frankly, he wasn't. Rather, it was simply because he was always selling.

As a kid, I remember folks saying to me: "That uncle of yours—wow, what a terrific guy!" In restaurants, the waiters all smiled—genuinely—when he walked in. Box-office attendants at movie theaters brightened when he came along. Every traffic cop who ever stopped him for a ticket left as his friend, and Larry drove off without the ticket.

He once told me his secret: "Just treat people like people. That's all it takes."

I said that my Uncle Larry was always selling, and that's obviously true. The interesting thing, though, is that he was *not* a salesman by profession—never sold a thing in his life.

Still, Uncle Larry was a real Selling Ace. I, for one, have always tried, at least, to follow his example.

Everybody's Favorite Salesman

Now let's get into the more specific factors that directly affect the image you create among your customers.

Notice I am not referring, here, to sales techniques. This has nothing to do with opening or closing any sale. These are simply the traits that will make you more *popular* with your customers.

But, as we all know, the guy who is everybody's favorite salesman is bound to get the most of everybody's business.

I conducted my own "Gallup poll" among several hundred top purchasing agents, and found that "everybody's favorite salesman" has seven prime qualities. Here are six of them:

1. *He is informed.* Here's that knowledge factor again! But, apparently, it can't be stressed too strongly. Buyers like salesmen who know what they're talking about. The salesman who knows his own business—and something about the prospect's—always seems to get the best hearing.

2. *He is helpful.* He doesn't seem to be strictly out for himself. The order doesn't appear to be his only interest. Buyers like salesmen who come up with new ideas to help *them*. This, of course, is just another definition of creative selling.

3. *He is cheerful.* Buyers don't like salesmen who are hysteri-

cally overenthusiastic, but they do appreciate optimism. Personal problems, if there are any, are left at home. It's far better to be chipper than to have a chip on the shoulder.

4. *He is fair.* This, I found out, is a three-edged sword. Naturally, any buyer wants a salesman to be fair to him. But he also likes the salesman who is fair and loyal to his own company—and not unfair to his competitors.

5. *He is truthful.* As I've pointed out before, most purchasing men are pretty smart apples. They can smell a liar a county away. Certainly, if a salesman does get by with any flimflam once, he won't get a chance to try again. The popular salesman always tells the truth, the whole truth, and nothing but.

6. *He's a gentleman.* He's nice to have around, but he knows enough not to stick around too long. He gets down to earth—he certainly isn't a stuffed shirt—but he's never vulgar. And, of course, he never gets mad. Everybody's favorite salesman always remains a gentleman.

Those, then, are the six preferred qualities possessed by all popular salesmen. They led the poll.

Except for one—the seventh—which was so outstandingly *the* most often-mentioned trait, as being so important in so many different ways, it needs special mention.

Here it is.

"You Can Depend on Me"

Right there you have five of the most powerful words in selling. Read 'em and rejoice!

If you can say those words to your customers—and mean them—you are immediately a front-running candidate for everybody's favorite salesman. Because *dependability* is the one truly vital personal quality of a popular salesman, according to the buyers I interviewed.

The well-liked salesman keeps his appointments, without forever straggling in late. When he says he's going to be at a certain place, at a certain time—barring war, flood, or other acts of God—he's there.

When a special request is made, the popular salesman *always* follows through. He doesn't hand out promises indiscriminately —when he does make a promise, he keeps it.

One of the best-liked advertising specialty men around New York is Irving Nissman, head of the Marvic Company in Brooklyn. Part of Marvic's success is undoubtedly due to the cleverness of the items themselves—some are truly unique. But a statement that Irv Nissman made to me one day reveals another vital clue to the results his firm has achieved:

"In our business we get some mighty weird requests. Everybody wants something different. Occasionally, when we have to turn 'em down, we make enemies. But when we say we're going to do something, we do it. Whatever we promise, we deliver. And that sort of reputation gets around."

Of course, everyone knows that Irv Nissman is the boss of his firm—which puts him a little closer to his own factory than you may be to yours. Whatever *he* says comes straight from the horse's mouth.

But remember this: to your customers, *you* are your company. When a promise is, or isn't, kept, they look to *you*. It's *your* reputation that's at stake.

Let 'em know they can depend on *you*.

Stay in the Spotlight

You can't build an image unless you're known. The more folks who know you, the larger the image.

So it's important to *increase* your reputation, as well as improve it.

My friend Vince Ashton, with no previous experience in the business, became a million-dollar-a-year insurance underwriter in less than two years—and that's some record. How did he do it? Largely by joining. Joining what? Just about everything.

He's active—and I mean active—in the New York Sales Executives Club, the Association of Advertising Men and Women, the Toastmasters' Club, the Queens County Grand Jurors Association, a midtown Manhattan health club, etc.,

etc., etc. In fact, Vince showed me his appointment book once. He's busier attending meetings than most of us are eating!

Vince Ashton is a real Selling Ace—largely because he stays in the spotlight.

Of course, perennial joiners can become mighty *un*popular if all they do during these extra-curricular activities is hand out business cards. This can act like a boomerang and completely destroy the popular image you're trying to build up. You have to take a sincere, active part in each organization you join.

But if you're ready to contribute time and effort, *any* club or association can be helpful to you. (F.B.I. take note: I'm *not* including the Communist Party.) Trade associations, service clubs, church groups, etc.—all enable you to help your fellow man, and yourself.

It pays to stay in the spotlight.

Chapter 31 in a Nutshell

1. Even when you're not selling—you are.
2. The customers' favorite salesman is the boss's favorite, too.
3. If they can depend on you, you can depend on their business.
4. They can't see you unless you're in the spotlight.

Chapter 32

CHARTING YOUR COURSE TO SUCCESS

Be Success-Minded

Well, we're coming down the home stretch. The book is almost ended.

But for you it's strictly the beginning. If, by this time, you have decided that you *will* "Sell Like an Ace," then you *will* "Live Like a King" from here on out.

So it should be a good idea right now to look ahead. And that's what I want to do with you during this last chapter.

The first thing you have to do is simply decide to be success-minded. Just *think* in terms of the success you want. Then *believe* your own thoughts. Wishing may not make it so, but it's undeniably a prime ingredient.

Remember this:

The world has never known a successful man who didn't believe he was *deserving* of that success. The world has seen plenty of men who believed they could do something—and then did it.

Ollie Evinrude believed he could devise something better than oars—and he started the fabulous outboard motor boat industry.

A guy named Birdseye believed there was something in frozen foods—and every kitchen in America is testimony to his vision.

Then there was a fellow called Henry Ford. He believed in something—and built an empire.

A couple of brothers named Wright believed that man could fly.

Before you get too carried away, I have just one word of caution: The means, as well as the end, must be justified.

A guy by the name of Adolf Hitler believed he could conquer the world—and didn't.

But without belief, we'd still be living in caves.

Plan All the Way to the Top

Here's something that has always amazed me: *nobody ever plans to fail, but many people do fail to plan.*

How about *you?* What are *your* plans?

We hear so often about so-and-so who "got the breaks"— and, certainly, luck plays a part in everyone's life.

But it's a funny thing. The breaks usually come to those who are *ready* for them. And the reason that some people are ready for lucky breaks is that they have a *plan.* They aren't just chosen—they're in line.

And here's the vital point: If you want to get to the top, you have to plan all the way. "Seek and ye shall find," says the Bible. Seek the mediocre and that's what you'll get. Seek the greatest and there it is.

Of course, we put a lot of emphasis on this in our Selling Aces Workshops. The folks in our classes *believe* in success, or they wouldn't be there.

In Session 12, we place special stress on planning ahead. Each person is asked to announce his goals for the future. And this is where the men are separated from the boys.

One fellow aims at raising his annual income from $6000 to $8000. Another dreams of being Regional Sales Manager. Another looks forward only to paying off his used car.

If I were to place a bet, I'd put my money on the guys who express their determination to hit the moon.

Because targets have a way of being hit.

If you aspire to mediocrity, you'll probably make it.

If you aim at the top, you may not quite—but if you don't aim, you certainly won't score.

The pinnacle belongs to those who try.

Hit from Where the Hand Is

With all this stuff about the big time, you may wonder if I'm talking strictly in the clouds. Planning all the way to the top is fine, you may say, but what about the here and now?

The answer is this: Hit from where the hand is.

Which is another way of saying that it's best to start at the beginning. Aim for the heights, but don't be afraid to trample in the lowlands first.

I remember a lecturer at my high school in Honolulu. "Whatever you do," he said, "do it better than anybody else."

And I think that's pretty good advice.

My friend Mel Vaught started with the J. J. Newberry Company as a stock-boy—and he was the best stock-boy in the store. He became manager of the store—and did a better job than other managers of other stores. He rose to Division Manager —and distinguished himself in that capacity.

At every level, up the ladder, Mel did the best job he knew how. That's why, today, he is Vice-President and a Director of Newberry's, one of the largest merchandising firms in the world.

He started by "hitting from where the hand is."

The moral is clear:

You may not be able to achieve total success today—but you can start.

Obstacles Are Inevitable

I've always felt sorry for the man without obstacles. And, yet, I know that's wrong—*everybody* runs into problems of one kind or another.

Certainly, you can't be a salesman without having a few downs along with the ups. But they needn't bother you, if you recognize that obstacles are inevitable.

Demosthenes, they say, had an impediment in his speech.

Milton, the great English poet, was blind; Beethoven was deaf.

Franklin D. Roosevelt, one of the most powerful men of the century, was a cripple.

All of which should prove that obstacles needn't stop you. They may hinder your progress, but they'll halt it only if you let them.

Here's a brief biography of another famous man:

'31—He failed in business.

'32—He was defeated for the legislature.

'33—Failed in business again.

'35—His sweetheart died.

'36—Nervous breakdown.

'40—Defeated for Elector.

'48—Defeated for Congress.

'55—Defeated for the Senate.

'56—Defeated for Vice-President.

'60—*Elected President of the United States!*

The man's name? Abraham Lincoln.

The Price of Privilege Is Service

However you want to take it, this is a sermon. I'm borrowing the title from one of my college professors, who ended his economics course the same way.

Because—in selling as in everything else—he profits most who contributes most.

Throughout this book, my aim has been to help you make more sales. And I hope I've succeeded—to some extent, at least—in that objective.

But, as Grantland Rice pointed out in his famous poem, there's something else that transcends the importance of any individual order: It's "how you play the game."

As a salesman, you are a vital cog in the machinery of the American economic system. For without salesmen, there are no sales. And without sales, businesses cannot live. So that makes you a pretty important guy.

The question for you is: How anxious are you to contribute?

Are you content to be an order-taker? To live off the deals that fall into your lap? Or do you *really* want to help your customers and your company?

Remember, the world has long rolled merrily along without you, and, no doubt, it could continue.

But if you do your part to help it roll more smoothly, then *you*—along with the world—will be the beneficiary.

Because the price of privilege is service.

"Sell Like an Ace—Live Like a King!"

But serve your fellow man along the way.

Chapter 32 in a Nutshell

1. Think it, believe it, do it.
2. Aim high enough—the higher you aim, the higher you hit.
3. The time to start is now. The place is here.
4. You may be down—but you're never out.
5. Successful selling is serving.

INDEX

189